The Paper Tiger's Daughters

D1738554

BETSY CHANG HA

DEDICATION

I dedicate this book to my daughters, Stephanie and Brittany, the third generation offspring of the Paper Tiger. We cannot change our past, but we can rewrite the story and shape the future with hope, compassion, and the strength of the tiger.

CONTENTS

ACKNOWLEDGMENTS

I like to express my deepest gratitude for my grandfather, Joseph Chang, for the foresight of documenting his memories of the Chang family from many generations before he passed away. He knew I would need the information to write this book one day. I am grateful to have my mother, Elsie Chang, spending hours on Face Time during the pandemic, sharing her memory of the Paper Tiger, and filling the gaps in my childhood memories. A special thank-you to my aunt, Pauline Yang, for sending forth an outline of the Jin family tree and events that helped me weave in Ching-Ma's family story. Finally, I want to express my gratitude for Co Ha and David Ha for helping me tell the story of their mother, Chi Buu Ly.

To Stephanie and Brittany, thank you for the privilege of being your mother in this life time. You have helped me see the intersectionality of multiple Asian American immigrants in our family, and inspired me to tell the story. I hope my personal lessons will inspire you to help heal and nurture our next generation with intentionality. We are better together.

I am grateful for crossing paths and partnering with health care leaders, like Dr. Terry Hill and Dr. Cristina Jose-Kampfner, advocating for the most marginalized population.

I am indebted to the scientific knowledge and publications on Adverse Childhood Experiences (ACEs) and trauma informed care that inspired me to share my story. My offering of the self-healing practices were based on formal yoga teachers training, my own daily practices, as well as trauma informed classes I developed for my students. I leveraged many invaluable resources by various teachers and authors in the research of this book, in particular:

1. *The Deepest Well: Healing the Long-Term Effects of Childhood Adversity* by Dr. Nadine Burke Harris, 2018.

2. *Relationship of Childhood Abuse and Household Dysfunction to Many Leading Causes of Death in Adults: the Adverse Childhood Experiences (ACE) Study*, by Dr. Vincent Felitti, Dr. Robert Anda, and colleagues, 1998.

3. *My Grandmother's Hands, Racialized Trauma to Mending Our Hearts and Bodies*, by Resmaa Menakem, 2017.

4. *The Proven Power of Being Kind to Yourself: Self-Compassion* by Kristin Neff, PhD, 2011.

5. Somatic Orientation, a term from Dr. Sam Himelstein based on Dr. Peter Levine (1977, 1997, 2010) work on Somatic Experiencing.

6. RAIN, acronym of a mindfulness practice coined by Tara Brach.

7. https://www.sfusd.edu/facing-our-past-changing-our-future-part-i-century-segregation-san-francisco-unified-school-district
8. https://www.prisonlegalnews.org/news/2006/mar/15/federal-court-seizes-california-prisons-medical-care-appoints-receiver-with-unprecedented-powers/
9. https://historydaily.org/ishi-the-last-wild-indian

Finally, A special thank you to Stephanie, for helping me proof read the final manuscript, so I can publish this book in the year of the tiger to honor the courage and strength of the tiger in each one of us.

Namaste.

1 PROLOGUE

∞ ♥ ∞

"Trauma is not destiny. It can be healed."

"When we heal our trauma, individually and collectively, we don't just heal our bodies. By refusing to pass on the trauma we inherited, we help heal the world."

- Resmaa Menakem

I am considered very privileged, because I am an American. I was spared from personally witnessing war or experiencing the life of a displaced refugee from country of birth as my ancestors and relatives. I always had food, shelter, clothing, and caring adults in my life. This story is

1

about the invisible impact of the intergenerational trauma and the epigenetic harm that unintentionally passed on to the next generation from our ancestors. This is my journey of deep self-healing from the shame of hidden family secrets. As I peeled away the malformed protective scars layer by layer I allowed myself to feel the pain in a safe healing place. My heart deepened with gratitude for the gift of resilience that prevailed through the generations. I hope this book will resonate with your soul, and shed lights on why we feel the way we do. Although we all have our own experience, I hope my story will help you and our future generations with tangible resources to continue mending our hearts and bodies. I am grateful for the publications of many neuropsychologists, medical professionals, researchers, yoga teachers, and healers, such as Dr. Peter Levine, Dr. Nadine Burke Harris, Dr. Tara Brach, Dr. Kristen Neff, Resmaa Menakem, Hala Khouri, and many more who opened my eyes to the neuroscience of trauma informed care in healing Adverse Childhood Experiences (ACEs). I have incorporated their collective wisdom and adapted tools that worked for me as resources in my own healing journey.

The Paper Tiger's daughter is my mother, who abandoned me when I was five years old, after my father abandoned us when I was three years old, simply because my sister and I were born girls. My perspective of the story was fuzzy and painful, until I became a mother. Then I reconnected with my own birth mother, heard her story, understood the political landscape of her era, and the choice she made within the cultural context of her time. I eventually learned to forgive. But still I can never forget. Now as a grown adult, mother, a survivor of generational trauma, and a life-long advocate for children's health and wellness, I believe we have the power to change the narrative with deep love and wisdom. It is my generation's responsibility to break the bondage of the past. We must help heal the epigenetic wounds, build resiliency, and eliminate systemic racism with compassion for the sake of our children and their children. Although this is my story told from multiple generational lenses, I weaved in my mother's perspective as the third daughter of the Paper Tiger of Shanghai, a rich girl turned refugee displaced from China to Taiwan, after the Communist took over their home in 1949. Asian American women and immigrants caught between old traditions, generational trauma, and displacement, our will to survive at all cost made us resilient.

The Deepest Well by Dr. Nadine Burke Harris was published in 2018. Reading the book was like an aha moment for me. The book eloquently summarized decades of scientific evidence linking ACEs to mental and physical health conditions of adults. Most importantly, the toxic stress of the traumatic events during early childhood can be ameliorated or reversed with just one stable, loving, and supportive adult presence and perhaps early psychosocial interventions. Based on the monumental ACEs studies published by Dr. Vincent Felitti, Dr. Robert Anda, and colleagues in 1997 linking ACEs to adult chronic conditions. Felitti and Anda sorted ACEs such as abuse, neglect, and house hold dysfunction in the following 10 categories:

1. Emotional abuse (recurrent)
2. Physical abuse (recurrent)
3. Sexual abuse (contact)
4. Physical neglect
5. Emotional neglect
6. Substance abuse in the household
7. Mental illness in the household
8. Mother treated violently
9. Divorce or parental separation
10. Criminal behavior in household (e.g., house member incarcerated)

The Felitti and Anda's ACEs study revealed strong correlation of dose-response relationship in the adult population. For example, a person with an ACE score of seven or more has triple the lifetime odds of getting lung cancer and three and a half time of the odds of ischemic heart attack.

The subsequent studies by Dr. Harris on children revealed that children with four or more ACEs were twice as likely to be overweight or obese or 32.6 times more likely to have learning and behavior problems.

As part of my improving racial health equity work during the COVID19 pandemic from 2020 to 2021, I came across Resmaa Menakem's book, *My Grandmother's Hands, Racialized Trauma and the Pathway to Mending Our Hearts and Bodies, published in 2017.* Although the book was focusing on the African Americans and White Americans experience in the United States in relation to the police professions, the insight of the white-body supremacy resonated with my experience as an Asian American. I gained a deeper understanding of how the white-body supremacy and the adoration of the European culture tinted my parents and grandparents upbringing before they arrive to the United States (US), the Beautiful Country, the land of the free and bountiful. Furthermore, I understood how the white-body supremacy defined an insidious standard of beauty for BIPOC (black, indigenous, and persons of colors) girls way before my time.

Menakem's book offered holistic strategies and experiential practices to process the "clean pain" and purge out the "dirty pain" in our bodies, so there is hope to stop the epigenetic harm of our multigenerational trauma to our future generations. Menakem adapted the term clean pain and dirty pain from his mentors, Dr. David Schnarch and Dr. Steven Hayer, both American licensed clinical psychologist and authors. Clean pain is defined as pain that mends and can build one's capacity for growth. To express clean pain requires honesty, vulnerability, and courage to step into the unknown for healing. Dirty pain is the pain of avoidance, blame, and denial. The dirty pain is rooted in one's most wounded self and often expressed through verbal, physical or emotional violence. The expression of dirty pain only creates more trauma and suffering for self and others. The healing of generational trauma starts with me and my generation. I am grateful for Menakem's Body and Breath Practices that help me personally be grounded to start this book. These self-healing activities were necessary during the writing of this book, and gave me the resources to feel safe as I excavated the generational trauma of an immigrant family.

My ACE score is seven, and my story is part of my own healing journey and a testimony of resiliency. This story written with love and compassion aims to help heal the epigenetic wounds and the multigenerational trauma that I unintentionally passed on to my children. The words of these pages represent building blocks to my own pathway of mending my own heart and body. As a trauma-informed certified yoga teacher, I practice what I teach. Purging of the trauma of ACEs is a life-long healing process. The Self-Healing Moments at the end of each chapter include my own trauma informed practices. Some of the practices came from the yoga classes I offered as a volunteer teacher at the 360 Youth Diversion to help stop the school to prison pipeline in my own community. My intention of this book is not replacing professional therapy, but simply offering a portal and tools for continuing release of the soul pain and creating space for deeper healing within my own body. Through the writing of this book, I learned to discern clean pain versus dirty pain in my own body with greater sensitivity and self- acceptance.

I hope my story will inoculate compassion, wisdom, and strength into our next generation. Despite my own pain and sufferings, I am deeply grateful for having the genetics of cross-generational resilience of strong women in my blood. May the hidden loving intention, behind the will to survive of our ancestors, provide wisdom to help our next generation to heal from the multi-dimensional toxic stress of their time, and be equipped to move forth with renewed hope for the future.

2 AWAKENING

∞ ♥ ∞

"Behind every strong woman lies a broken little girl who

had to learn how to get back up and never depend on any

one."

-Unknown

" I am beautiful, bountiful, blissful, and bright!" I smile at the image of myself in the mirror every morning with my new mantra. I choose to be content with life being perfectly imperfect today. Learning to love my self and be content is daily practice and a lifelong journey. I spent half a century looking for the missing puzzle piece that I thought I needed to make my life whole. It was an addiction to constantly striving to fill the void of feeling not good enough. I was meticulously groomed to be the "model minority" as a child of an immigrant family, and I fitted the mold quite well. But I always felt something was missing, and I never felt I belong anywhere.

I was born in Taiwan in the late 1950's, a part of the Baby Boomer generation. Sometimes I have memories and I am unsure if they are real or just dreams. I remember looking through a wooden crib as a baby - I do not know exactly how young I was. But the distinct feeling of being left alone was somatic. I also remember being lost as a very young child, perhaps two years old, wandering in a busy open market searching for my mother. I continued to experience frequent dreams into adulthood, the same scenario of getting lost and cannot find a way out. Even in the adult body, I felt the child's body tensing from breath-holding spells in reaction to the emotional pain of abandonment. I also recall vignettes of adventures, memories of me standing on the front of a scooter, with my father driving and my mother riding on the back while pregnant with my sister. I can feel the humid tropical wind on my face flying through the streets of Taipei, I can still hear the monsoon rains pouring down in buckets as a little child ran for shelter through the brick courtyard in quick short steps. It was like watching a movie whenever these images appeared in my dreams.

∞ ♥ ∞

I remember Elsie Chang, my mother, as a beautiful, loving, and easy going mom who always worked outside of the home, unlike most mothers of her era. She was educated at a private British school in Shanghai, graduated from an elite girls' school in Taipei, and spoke fluent English. She always worked for American companies in Taiwan. Elsie was recognized as the "school flower" in college for her delicate beauty. She fell in love with a handsome playboy, Robert Chang (Both Changs from Shanghai). My mother referred to Robert as Bob. They crossed paths on the college campus. Robert was on his Vespa as Elsie rode her bicycle across the campus. He instantly noticed her and became determined to get to know her. They formally met at an inter-university mixer dance. The main reason for their marriage was because of their common upbringing in Shanghai - both families idolized the western culture. It was 門當戶對, Mén-dāng-hù-duì, a "Marriage of Matching Doors," by Chinese tradition. In 1955, Bob and Elsie married after one year of engagement. Two years later, they gave birth to me. Although I had a Chinese name officially and later used it in school, everyone on both sides of the Chang family called me Betsy. Later I found out from my mother that I was named after the popular Betsy Wetsy doll because I was born with a full head of hair, big round eyes, and a tiny mouth like the doll.

I was treated like a doll, a play toy for my mother

instead of a real baby. When I was only two years old, My mother started to perm my hair with Tony solution to make my hair curly like Shirley Temple, a popular American child actress, a pop star adored by the fans in Asia for her singing and dancing talents. My mother always dressed me up with different western style outfits including expensive saddle shoes from the US. I would accompany my fashionable mother to parties with her American friends. I was the play doll with curly hair in a frilly dress, an implicit American standard of cuteness instead of a Chinese baby born with a full head of straight black hair. I learned at a very young age that the external image of a girl was very important, and the standard of beauty was based on the white bodies we saw in the American movies. When you were born as a girl with no value, how pretty you looked externally marked your worth in the traditional Chinese family.

Self-Healing Moment

Anchoring Practice

Grounding

- Sit up tall.
- Place both feet on the ground and both hands on your lap.
- Turn your head slowly from side to side, look around your space, register where you are right now.

Check in

- Take a moment to Check In - notice how you are feeling: what is the state of your mind today? Find a word to describe it.
- Soften your gaze or close your eyes.
- Give yourself permission to be here now.

Body Awareness

- Notice how your mind starts to settle down in this quietness.
- Bring your awareness to the bottom of your feet, wiggle your toes, and plant them back down on to the floor.

- Find a sense of grounding, a sense of rooting down and connecting with the earth beneath you.
- Feel the connection of the back of the chair supporting you.
- Lengthen your torso evenly from the base of your spine towards the crown of your head.
- Maintain a long spine.
- Lift your heart and roll your shoulders up, back and down a few times.
- Maintain this alert but relaxed position.
- Soften your face.
- Unclench your jaw.
- Invite a gentle smile to your face.

Breath Awareness

- Bring your awareness to your breath - just observe it without changing it for a few breath cycles.
- Start to scan your body with your breath from the top of your head to the bottom of your feet.
- Notice any sensations, any constriction or tightness.
- (Note: If this practice up to this point is already too much for you to process, STOP. Just breathe or return to grounding.)
- Direct your breath to parts of your body that need a little softening.

- We can't force our bodies to relax or release tension, but we can direct our breath to the areas of our bodies that are tense. Simply invite some softness and gently let go.
- We have innate resources to heal ourselves with each breath cycle, so breathe deeply.

3 THE PAPER TIGER'S DAUGHTER

∞ ♥ ∞

"Let me not mar that perfect dream

By an auroral stain,

But so adjust my daily night

That it will come again."

-Emily Dickinson

The western influence and white body adoration of my ancestors came from Shanghai, decades before my parents immigrated to the United States (US) to realize the American dream. Elsie Chang, my mother was the sole family member who opened the path for her larger Chang family members to immigrate to the United States (US). She did this through her second marriage to a third generation Hawaiian Chinese American as a rebound of a heart break of her first marriage to Robert Chang.

Elsie was born in the early 1930's to the Chang family of Shanghai, a family known for its wealth and western connections. My maternal grandfather, Charles Chang, was a dapper young man with three wives, one official wife and two concubines. At age of thirty, Charles' father put him on the opulent Queen Mary cruise ship headed to US and Europe to establish business connections, so he would eventually takeover his father's European paper import business. High quality paper products, such as wall paper from France and Great Britain was in high demand by the bourgeois Shanghai society starting in the 1400's. Later the Chang company supplied paper to the Qing dynasty to print paper currencies. Charles Chang was famously referred to as the Shanghai's 紙老虎, Zhǐ-lǎo-hǔ "Paper Tiger" for his influential position behind the powerful monopoly of the fine paper industry. Later the "Paper Tiger" expression became well known internationally as a slogan used by Mao Zedong, leader of the People's Republic of China, against the US government. The Chinese Communist Party used the literal term in a derogatory manner to undermine the US power and claim of threats to the communist regime as bluff and ineffectual.

Elsie was the third daughter to Charles Chang's

first wife. She was a cute baby and resembled her grandfather's favorite concubine; hence, Elsie was always favored and lavished with affections. In contrary with the fourth daughter Joyce, Elsie's younger sister, who was not as cute as her older sisters, was ignored by her own mother. My mother told me the sad story that the nanny would apply red lipstick and rouge on her baby sister Joyce and dress her in pretty silk for mother's morning kiss. Her mother would simply wave the nanny away without any desire to hold her own baby daughter.

However the Chang family embraced the western traditions, they actually treated daughters the same as the sons with private English school educations. I learned that my Auntie Jean, the oldest daughter, was allowed to wear trousers, take piano, riding lessons, and drove an automobile at the age of sixteen. At a very young age, the Chang daughters were included in society functions with the westerners. As young as the age of thirteen, dressed in the latest French fashions, Elsie often tagged along with her parents and older sister to the Country Club that only the whites or the wealthy Chinese were allowed to enter. The lavish life style of the elite Chinese business class and the corrupted Qing Empire were the target of the Communist movement in China.

Under the weakness and corruption of the Qing dynasty, the last dynasty of the imperial China, the British and American enclaves in Shanghai merged in the year 1863, forming the Shanghai International Settlement, in which the British subjects and American citizens would enjoy extraordinary and consular jurisdiction under the terms of treaties signed by the weak Qing dynasty. Later the Nationalist Party or Kuomintang repudiated these treaties in 1943.

As children of a well to do Chinese family growing up in the French Concession of the Shanghai International Settlement, my mother was sheltered from the atrocities of the war and the suffering of the ordinary Chinese people. She re-called as a little girl peering over the villa balcony in the evening and watching the city being bombed by the allies as watching entertaining fireworks. She did not have the faintest idea of the suffering of people who looked like her beyond the artificial safety and boundaries of Shanghai International Settlement. The government corruption and wealth inequality fueled the uprising of the people. Since the Nationalist Party led by Chiang Kai-Shek represented the wealthy Chinese who admired the western culture, they were eventually over turned by the Communist Party under Mao Zedong.

As the situation worsen in China, it became obvious that Communist Party was winning and the takeover was imminent. By that time Charles Chang, my grandfather, had already established a household for his favorite second wife in Taiwan. The first wife finally agreed reluctantly to leave their comfortable life in Shanghai. The Chang family hastily sold their Shanghai villa in the French Concession to a business partner and Communist sympathizer for thirty gold bars. The Chang family fled to Taiwan in 1949 on the last ship to Taiwan. Per Elsie's recollection, her mother had all intention of staying in Taiwan for a few months as a long summer vacation, and return back to Shanghai once the political situation calmed down. Hence, they only took a small suit case with light summer outfits, matching white shoes, and salted fish as travel snacks. My mother recalled, the situation was chaotic at the harbor, crowded with Chinese people fleeing the country in desperation. She felt fearful for the first time in the midst of the mob. The anxious crowds were fighting to embark the ship, so a man servant cleverly decided to hoist my mother and her younger siblings through the ship's kitchen window to protect them from the panicking mob. Since my grandmother was a plump lady, she had to board the ship with other passengers. Little did they know that was a trip of no turn, all would be lost to the Communist government.

As a pampered son of a wealthy family, our maternal grandfather, the Paper Tiger, was very trusting of other people and never had to manage his own money; he quickly lost all the gold and properties through poor investments and dishonest business associates. All three wives had to be dispersed and lived on meager resources separately. That traumatic childhood experience of losing their comfortable home, carefree life style, and societal standing due to the war, caused my mother to always value money beyond people. Luckily that both Jean and Elsie had western education and spoke perfect English. Right after college, they found work with the airline company and American mission organization respectively. They were able to help their parents and younger brothers finish primary and higher education in Taiwan.

∞ ♥ ∞

Elsie met Robert, my father, at a dance party. It was love at first sight. They were both great dancers and were a lovely couple on the dance floor. Elsie was delighted to discover that they can converse in Shanghainese and shared fond memories of childhood in Shanghai. After courting and one year of engagement, my mother married my father. They lived in a small house and adopted the American way of a modern nuclear family.

In the traditional Chinese culture, girls were not valued. Especially in my paternal grandmother's house hold. There was only one son for each generation. Starting as a newlywed, my mother was already under tremendous pressure from my paternal grandmother, her mother-in law, to produce a son. My mother had a very difficult birth, and I was immediately admitted to the neonatal intensive care unit (NICU) with difficulty breathing, likely pneumonia due to meconium aspiration during the long birthing process. My paternal grandmother refused to see me or help pay for the month long hospitalization. I was told by my aunts later on that my grandmother actually said: "Let her die, just a girl..." My father recently completed mandatory military services and was unemployed at the time, he had to sell his blood to pay for the hospital bills. My maternal grandmother found out about this, and stopped speaking to my paternal grandmother. The animosity between the two Chang families started from my birth.

Two and a half year later, my sister was born, she was given the name Judy for a very specific reason. You see, the English pronunciation of Judy sounded exactly like 求弟, "begging for a brother" in Chinese. My father never visited my mother in the hospital, and he was sent to US on a student VISA shortly after the birth of his second daughter.

My mother never shed a tear, at least I have never seen her cry. Ironically, as the favorite daughter of the Paper Tiger, she had to live under the same roof with a mother-in-law who was born in the year of the tiger and was known as the Tiger Lady, who ruled the Chang house hold with cunningness and an iron fist.

Self-Healing Moment

Grounding and Breathing

- Find a quiet place to sit.
- Use your breath as an anchor to stay in the present moment.
- Feel your breaths move in and out of your body.
- Notice the slight pulse between your inhale and exhale.
- Notice what is happening with your thoughts while you are in perfect stillness.
- Allow and accept the normalcy of finding your thoughts wandering while your body is in perfect stillness.
- Return to your breaths or the rise and fall of your belly.
- Accept the fact that your breath is always in the present moment.
- Breathe in and breathe out.
- Did your mind wandered to the present or the past?
- With no judgement or attachment, simply turning right back to the next breath.
- Breathe in and breathe out.
- Without latching on to the thoughts or feelings.

- Choose not to get on the next train of thoughts, stay with your breath.

4 THE TIGER LADY

∞ ♥ ∞

"Why can't you give the respect that I'm entitled to?"

-Joan Crawford from Mommie Dearest Film

We called my paternal grandmother, 親媽 Ching-Ma in Shanghainese. Ironically it is translated to English as "Mommie Dearest." She was born under the Chinese zodiac sign of the tiger, and people called her the Tiger Lady behind her back. She was powerful, independent and cunning with a distinct presence of authority. Everyone in the family was terrified of her. Although she did not have any formal higher education, she was street smart and business-minded. If she was born in today's society, I could see her as a successful business woman, perhaps a c-suite executive in a publicly traded company. She definitely had the grit.

Ching-Ma's father, my paternal great grandfather, Jin Shi-Lin, was a well-to-do authoritative man with high ranking government post with the Qing dynasty. Later the surname of Jin, the Chinese word for gold, was translated to King in English, as his offspring studied abroad. Ching-Ma became Nancy King when she immigrated to the US. My paternal great grandfather had eight wives, one legal wife plus seven concubines. He had seven sons and nine daughters. He was able to send three sons to study abroad. First wife's son graduated from Harvard University of US; second wife or first concubine's first son graduated from Columbia University of US, and the second son graduated from Imperial University of Japan. Ching-Ma was the second child of the third concubine, she had an older brother and two younger sisters. When Ching-Ma was sixteen years old, her mother died of a cervical infection, a condition that could be cured with antibiotic, if she was permitted to seek medical help. Considering the infection was located in the female reproductive part of the body, the old tradition would not allow her to be seen by any male physician for fear of shame. So for the family, saving face was more important than saving my great grandmother's life.

Ching-Ma had to grow up quickly and exercise her wit in order to survive the competitions between siblings, especially from other scheming concubines, all vying for the attention from her authoritative father. She benefitted from the Western influence of the time, for example she was spared from foot binding as other typical Chinese girls born of the upper class families. Foot binding was a Chinese custom started in the Tang dynasty for the sole purpose of creating tiny feet that was consider attractive and distinguished these girls as upper classes. The bound foot was called Lotus Foot, 蓮花足 Liánhuā zú. The women with bound foot had a very distinct sway of the hip as they walk, and that was considered very attractive to the men of upper classes. Foot-binding required breaking the bones in girls' feet at a very young age between five to eight years old. Typically the binding was done by an elder woman of the family or a professional foot binder. The binding of the broken foot would continue through a monthly cycle of extremely painful process, alternating between removing the bind to allow healing of the ulceration or infection, and increasing the tightening of the foot with long strips of cloth after the ulcers healed. It was common for these girls' toes to necrotize from gangrene. The inhuman torture of the girl would continue until she reached early teens or when she stopped growing after puberty. The foot binding process aimed to create a perfectly shaped tiny foot no longer than three inches. Foot binding was also a way to control girls, especially strong-will girls, to prevent them from running away. The Lotus Foot added value to these girls and made them better prospects for marriage. Unfortunately, foot binding became a way for the lower class families to improve their social class by binding their daughter's feet. Especially when a girl was born with a pretty face, a small Lotus Foot would improve her prospect of becoming a rich man's concubine, and the girl's family would gain social standing or some fortune from the arrangement. Sadly, the custom of foot binding continued through the early 20th century. I wonder how many of these girls with severe adverse childhood experience of foot binding ever healed from their years of trauma, and how generational trauma of girls impacted their capacity to be a loving and caring mother to their daughters?

Imagining my ancestors' experience of foot binding was more difficult than I had anticipated as I researched the mechanical process of foot binding. I remember growing up in Taiwan, occasionally seeing elderly women on the street with tiny feet, the sentiment as a child was simply curiosity. I also learned about the foot binding practice in the history books. But I have never witnessed the foot binding process or seen any Lotus Foot in the flesh. When I wrote this section from my ancestors' perspective, I felt my heart tightening and my throat constricting. I almost felt the terror and trauma of my ancestors who went through foot binding as very young girls. I had to stop writing, pulse, and take few deep breaths. I gave myself a safe space to process what was happening within my body. By now, I have a habit of practicing RAIN, a mindfulness meditation framework developed by Tara Brach, an American psychologist and well known teacher of meditation. I will share more about the RAIN practice in the later chapters. RAIN meditation starts by *Recognizing* what was happening within, and *Allowing* the sensation to bubble up without any resistance or judgement. As I *Investigating* the source of these new sensations in my body, I felt the release of my ancestors' trauma in the form of warm tears streaming down my face. I imagined myself reaching back in time and hugging these terrified young girls. Finally, *Nurturing* the part of me that was part of them with self-compassion. After the RAIN, I noticed gradual softening of my heart with deep gratitude, acceptance, and love for the girls of my ancestors.

I am so grateful that Ching-Ma was spared from the excruciating trauma of foot binding. Fortunately, she was also favored by her father because she demonstrated aptitude for mathematics. Hence, her father assigned her the responsibility of administrative book keeping for the family business. Nevertheless, as the daughter of a deceased concubine, my grandmother had to be strong to compete with the legal wife and the favoritism of more beautiful concubines. She learned very early as a young woman to be charming, cunning, and manipulative of people, especially men of power. She was a survivor.

My great-grandfather had a party where he invited the entire province. My future grandfather, Joseph Chang, attended the party on behalf of the Chang family. My great-grandfather was impressed with my future grandfather's beautiful calligraphy and education in literature. So my great-grandfather arranged for one of his daughters to marry my grandfather. An important step before the traditional marriage in China, was to check the match of the eight characters 八字 Bāzì, the birth chart between a man and a woman. Despite the fact that my grandparents' eight characters 八字 Bāzì did not match, my Ching-Ma was picked because of her experience of managing her father's household. Ironically, my paternal great grandmother, who herself had Lotus Foot and could not walk about freely, needed a capable daughter-in-law who could travel to the country side to collect rent, and be helpful to the family. My Ching-Ma was actually in love with another man at the time and never loved my grandfather. But as a woman in the old Chinese society, she had no say in the marriage. Ching-Ma married my grandfather at age seventeen. She also endured the oppressive mother-in-law, who demanded a son to continue Chang's single son lineage.

Eventually Ching-Ma became the matriarch of the family and carried on the same demands she experienced to her future daughters-in-law. During the Second Sino-Japanese War, Ching-Ma was sent by her mother-in-law to the country side to collect rent from the farmland owned by the Chang family. Ching-Ma told us that she had to travel alone by train to the remote villages, and was almost raped by a Japanese soldier had the conductor not intervened and saved her. She personally witnessed the atrocities of the war under the bloody Japanese occupation. Even though she detested Japanese due to the Second Sino-Japanese war, she frequently accompanied her sister to Japan and socialized in the success business circle after US defeated Japan. I remember seeing many artifacts from the Hiroshima atomic bomb site as decorations in our home in Taiwan.

∞ ♥ ∞

Ever since I can remember as a young child, when I was around my Ching-Ma, the feeling in my body was fear like a heavy brick on my chest. You have to be on the best behavior. She never hugged or kissed her children or grand-children. In fact, we were disciplined regularly by a spanking of our little hands with the bamboo stick of the feather duster, especially when our mother was at work. That was the traditional Chinese way to bring up well behaving children. My mother was often scolded for spoiling her children. I learned quickly to observe adults' moods by the color of their face, or 臉色 Liǎn-sè, so I can quickly adjust my own behaviors accordingly. A survival skill saved me from getting in trouble and served me well in the future. I was often praised by adults as the most obedient child and 聽話 Tīng-huà, good listener of words. My younger sister Judy, had the worse experience. She had severe asthma, in hindsight it may be related to neglect since infancy and my mother's experience of the toxic stress during her pregnancy. Judy got more beating by Ching-Ma for crying often because of her asthma symptoms. Ching-Ma blamed Judy for all the mis-fortune of the family, because my innocent sister was not a boy as they anticipated . My mother would hold Judy all night to sleep or lean her over the hot water steam to clear her lung, so my baby sister would not cry to awaken the household. Next morning, my mother would get up early, make sure we are dressed and in best behaviors, then she would catch a bus to work in the morning. Since my father was a student abroad with no steady income, Ching-Ma expected my mother to support us financially. My mother had to give her full salary to Ching-Ma every month to support her two young children and pitch in to support the larger household. My mother re-called at one point she was short on cash before the pay day, she had to borrow money from her sister to buy formula for us. Ching-Ma refused to help because we were worthless girls. In her mind, this was how she was treated as a daughter of a third concubine of the King family. You better learn on your own how to survive. Ching-Ma, although never had higher education, she was smart and possessed an elegant commanding presence. Ching-Ma learned to use these attributes very wisely. She expected no less from her daughters and granddaughters.

Many emotionally traumatic events directly affected my parents during that time that influenced the choices they made later, and how these choices eventually adversely impacted the subsequent generations.

Self-Healing Moment

Feeing Safe and Protected

- Take three cleansing breaths.
- Breathe in deeply and breathe out slowly and smoothly.
- Feel your feet connecting to the earth.
- Allow your body to soften and be fully supported.
- Close your eyes or soften your gaze.
- Bring to your mind a person, an animal, or any image of a being that makes you feel safe.
- Imaging that this being of your mind's eye is beside you at this moment, and you are in a safe place.
- Breathe in and breathe out effortlessly.
- Notice any constriction or discomfort in your body and allow the energy of your person, animal or being to help you feel secure and safe.
- Breathe and experience the sensation of safety and security of this moment.
- Imprint that sensation of feeling safe in your body.

5 THE PAPER TIGER'S GRANDDAUGHTER

∞ ♥ ∞

"As children, we don't have any definition of love as an abstract concept;

we just live love. It's the way we are."

-Don Miguel Ruiz

I did not learn about my parents' stories until adulthood. All I remember was being abandoned as a child and feeling unworthy. It was a summer day, I was five years old, coming home from school. As I innocently skipped through the door, I was immediately told by my aunt, who was wiping away her tears, that my mother left us. I was puzzled. I ran to the room that my sister and I shared with my mother. I opened the closet and drawers one-by-one to see for myself. I realized that all my mother's belongings were gone. To this day, I can still smell vividly the almond scent of her favorite Jergens lotion lingering in those empty spaces. All I had was the scent of my mother as tears were streaming down my little face. She was gone. But why? A child's mind could not understand.

Whenever I re-call that childhood scene, even as a woman in my sixties, my eyes still burn and well up with warm tears. I still could feel the knots in my throat and heaviness in my heart. Although painful, allowing the clean pain to flush out of my being is a necessary healing process to stop generational trauma. I compare this psychological healing process at the physical level as debridement of a poorly healed wound. The old wound may be so deep that it might have already formed a superficial scar on the surface of the skin. In order to allow growth of new healthy tissues, the wound must be thoroughly debrided and all the infected dead tissues removed. If the wound is not cleansed properly, the infection will return or the issues will eventually turn necrotic or dead. And sometimes the debriding process is too painful to bear. I know the analogy may be too graphic for readers with no health care background, but it is the only way I can describe it as a nurse. I had to pause here, take a deep breath and check in. At that point of my childhood, I disappeared from my body. Today I understand the psychological term of the trauma response called "dissociation."

∞ ♥ ∞

My parents were only married for four years when my father left to US. They were both twenty six years old. The long distance marriage did not last long. Considering the immigration law in the US at the time, they were destined to be apart. My father was a very handsome man and he was quite popular among the young Asian Americans social circle in Washington DC. As a womanizer, he fell for an attractive and older Japanese American divorcee. They were already having an affair when my father wrote a letter begging my mother to sign the divorce paper as a favor to help him stay in the US. Under a student VISA, the foreign students were not allowed to work. Deportation was inevitable if caught by the US Immigration and Custom Enforcement (ICE) agency during surprise raids. Since my father was under the pressure to send money back to Taiwan to support his parents, siblings, and children, he worked illegally in restaurants. He already had a few close calls with immigration raids. To be deported back to Taiwan would be shameful and a disgrace for the family. He told my mother that he had to marry an American citizen in order to become a permanent US resident and stay legally. At the time, my mother did not know her husband already had an affair with another woman and was expecting a child. My mother thought signing the paper will help her husband and it was a temporary arrangement.

Ching-Ma knew about the scheme. Despite the displeasure of having a Japanese daughter-in-law, considering the flashbacks of the Second-Sino-Japanese War and the bloody Japanese occupation of China experienced by my grandparents, Ching-Ma supported the divorce secretly hoping that the pregnancy with the second wife would produce a boy heir for the Chang family. When my mother found out the truth, she was devastated by the betrayal.

The law of the land, and consistent with Chinese tradition, the children belonged to the father's family. Hence the women had no custody right or entitlement for any financial support post-divorce. It was actually a disgrace to be a divorcee in Chinese culture. A stigma more severely judged for women than men. Ching-Ma forced my mother to leave without her children. Later I learned that in order for Ching-Ma to support my father's new marriage, he had to increase his financial support for both of us as well as for his parents and siblings in Taiwan. Since she no longer had the salary contribution from my mother. As the only one son, it was his filial duty to send US dollars to Ching-Ma monthly. My mother left her children behind quietly in 1962 with a broken heart and the stigma of a divorcee. She was forever criticized and judged harshly by my extended family members, even to this day, especially by those who grew up in the US, as a mother who was heartless and abandoned her children. No one knew or cared about her side of the story. We grew up pitied by relatives and family friends as unworthy and unwanted daughters raised by grandparents. It felt like everyone in the town of Beitau knew about my parents' divorce. Because of my mother's disgraceful circumstances, her family encouraged her to re-marry immediately. Fortunately, my mother was fluent in English and beautiful, she had a way out. At the age of twenty nine, Elsie accepted an arranged marriage to a much older Hawaiian Chinese American bachelor. She married six months after leaving her children to the Tiger Lady. I did not see my mother until many years later.

Self-Healing Moment

Somatic Orientation

- Find a quiet and private place.
- Sit comfortably.
- Look around you and behind you slowly.
- Notice three objects in your space.
- Notice two sounds you hear in your surroundings, name them.
- Notice how you are feeling, find one word to describe it.
- Find a sense of grounding with both feet on the floor.
- Give yourself the permission to be here now.
- Breathe in deeply and breath out slowly.
- Give yourself a hug, tell yourself you are safe now.
- Check in again, notice how do you feel? Name it and sit with it.
- Notice if there is anything else lingering in your body that no longer serve you.
- Shake them off or dance.

6 TRAUMA OF OUR ANCESTORS

∞ ♥ ∞

"We should feel sorrow, but not sink under its oppression."

-Confucius

I call my paternal grandfather 大爹 Du-Diaa, a term of endearment meaning "Big Daddy" in Shanghainese. He was a gentle and quiet man, unlike most Chinese men, he never spoke against his wife or even raise his voice in her presence. We later learned that my grandfather allowed my grandmother the freedom to do anything she desired as long as she stayed married to him. Their unhappy marriage eventually turned my grandfather into an alcoholic. I later learned from my youngest aunt, because my grandfather loved children, he rather stay in a loveless marriage than to see his children grow up in a broken marriage. He believed a divorce would bring shame to his family and disappoint his ancestors. When he became intoxicated with alcohol, he would hold on to his youngest daughter and sob for hours. My grandparents had an "open marriage" arrangement. It was an extremely progressive concept before its time. Ching-Ma was given all the freedom to have lovers, and eventually having a permanent domestic partner living with us as the "grand-uncle." Growing-up, I always thought it was perfectly normal to have many grandfathers and granduncles as a big family. We had dinners together as a big happy family.

My grandfather was the only son of the Chang family. Everyone has its own origin, and Du-Diaa actually came from a long lineage of generational childhood trauma. My grand aunt, who was also educated in English schools had to stay behind in the Communist China to take care of her aging mother, my great-grandmother. As representation of China's elderly and intellectual class, they personally endured harassment and witnessed the burning of the Chang family's official ancestor book from many generations during the Cultural Revolution of China in 1966. When Du-Diaa learned about the sad news, he swallowed the family pride and took the humiliation silently. Over the years, through Du-Diaa's recollection, he tried to reconstruct his ancestor's story starting with the Cao-Chang Orphan, who was born seven generations before Du-Diaa's birth. I am forever grateful for Du-Diaa's

Brief of Chang's Family History which he compile by memory before he passed away.

∞ ♥ ∞

Our Chang's family story started during a warfare between clans in China around the 1600's, every member of the original Chang family were slaughtered, leaving an orphan boy. The Cao family without a male heir, adopted this orphan as a successor of the Cao family. For generations, the Cao family lived in the town of Fahua, at the western part of Shanghai. According to the old Chinese traditions, the successors of the adopted son, after three generations, can resume their former surname. Hence the Chang family resumed as Cao-Chang family in gratitude to the Cao family for saving their only survivor of the historical warfare between clans. When Du-Diaa's great-great-grandfather resumed as a member of the Chang family, he moved to Zhenru, where he re-established the Chang's ancestor residence for generations. The house in Fahue was eventually converted into Cao-Chang family's ancestry temple. Every year during Qingming festival, Chinese Ancestor Memorial Day, the halls would be opened for memorial services held by Clan elders and descendants of different branches of the Cao-Chang family. Du-Diaa's great grandfather was a teacher, he had four sons and two daughters. During the Taiping Rebellion or Taiping Heavenly Movement, a revolt against the Qing dynasty in China in mid 1800's, Du-Diaa's grandfather and granduncle were teenagers. Two of them were captured by the soldiers to serve as slaves in the camp kitchen. When the soldiers came back to kidnap the third son, Du-Diaa's great grandfather knelt down and begged for his third son be spared from slavery. The third son was left behind and witnessed his father murdered under the merciless swords of the soldiers. The perpetuation of ACEs and epigenetic trauma continued during the turbulent time of the Taiping Rebellion from 1850 to 1864 which eventually proved unsuccessful, but still led to the death of more than 20 million Chinese.

Knowing the direct epigenetic impact of ACEs and generational trauma, I gained a better understanding of the poor mental and physical health of my great grandfather and his off-spring including my own father. Gaining the insight of what happened to our ancestors, opened my heart with compassion with the unforeseen capacity for forgiveness for all those who harmed me.

Self-Healing Moment

Ocean Breath

- Find a quiet place to rest on your back.
- Take a moment to check in - notice how you are feeling, what is the state of your mind today? Find a word to describe in.
- Soften your gaze or close your eyes if you choose.
- Give yourself the permission to be here now.

Body Awareness

- Notice how your mind starts to settle down in stillness.
- Bring your awareness to your back body, find a sense of grounding connecting with earth supporting you.
- Let go of any effort of holding yourself together.
- Let go just a tad with each natural breath.

Breath Awareness

- Connect with your breaths.
- Breathe in deeply and breath out slowly and smoothly.
- Imagine your breaths as ocean waves.

- As the cool wave washing over your body with each inhale, notice the calm.
- As the wave and receding with each exhale, allow it to carry away any thoughts or sensation that no longer serve you, notice the lightness.
- Allow yourself to enter a meditative state with the rhythm of the ocean breath, tapping into our innate resources of healing.
- Stay with the waves as long as you desire.
- Slowly come back to the present moment at your own pace.
- Inhale and stretch your body from your fingers to your toes.
- Exhale and hug your knees to your chest.
- Gently roll over to your side and rest in a fetal position.
- Rest there for few more breaths.
- Check in with yourself again, notice how you are feeling, find a word to name it.
- Pressing back up to a seated position.
- Notice the shift in your being.

7 LOVE IS KINDNESS

∞ ♥ ∞

"Love is patience, love is kind. It does not envy, it does not boast, it is not proud."

I Corinthian 13:4

Du-Diaa was not just my adoring grandpa, he filled the gap of mother and father. Even when he struggled with alcoholism, he was a kind drunk. He came from the lineage of only one son for each generation since his grandfather. His father was the only one son. He was prematurely born to Du-Diaa's grandmother, who had a weak physique and did not have adequate milk to nurse her son. Hence Du-Diaa's father grew up with poor health. During the Qing dynasty, under the influence of the Imperial Examination System, all professions were considered inferior to being officials of the Imperial court. Despite the fact that Du-Diaa's grandfather was a successful businessman, he pushed his son to be a "dragon" and succeed in a career as an official. Hence great emphasis was on pushing my great-grandfather to studying and passing the Imperial Examination with little attention to improve his physical health. When my great grandfather was sixteen, he passed the Imperial Examination at the county level. As an obedient filial son, he continued to study hard and passed the Imperial Exam at the highest provincial level, achieving the ranking of the juren, and gaining gentry status with social, political, and economic privileges.

Du-Diaa's first grandmother could not get pregnant after trying for ten years. Eventually she stopped menstruating all together from taking too much herbal medication of yin-nature. In the old Chinese tradition, to have no heir was considered unfilial of a descendent to their ancestor. Hence Du-Diaa's first grandmother dutifully obeyed her mother-in-law and agreed for her husband to marry a second wife for the sole purpose of producing an heir. Great grandmother Huang remained in charge of the household and was fondly referred by Du-Diaa as Du-Ma, the big mother. Du-Ma was a wise lady. Under the pretense of a supportive wife, she offered to personally search and pick a second wife for her husband. In order to maintain her standing as the first wife and the favorite of her husband, Du-Ma intentionally selected a very plain and uneducated woman from a farm as the second wife.

The second wife of my great grandfather became the biological mother of Du-Diaa. Unfortunately, Du-Ma picked a woman with very sad adverse childhood experiences, and she was also illiterate. My paternal great grandmother had a tragic experience before she married my great grandfather. Her mother died when she was a young child. One day her older sister took her shopping in town. Her sister forgot something at home, asked her little sister to wait at the street corner, while she ran home to fetch the forgotten item. Du-Diaa's biological mother was kidnapped by a human trafficker and was sold to a pig farmer family as a foster daughter. Later her foster mother gave birth to her own children, and so my great grandmother became a maid to the foster family. When she was nineteen, she was sold to the Chang family to be the second wife to my great grandfather, who was twenty-nine years of age. Unintentionally the Chang family introduced another source of ACE trauma and insidious epigenetic change to the future generation through this union. For the first six years, my great grandfather was confined to bedrest from a curious liver disease. By the time he recovered, the Imperial Examination had been abolished. Hence, my great grandfather was sent to Japan to study at the Meiji University. After he returned, he became a teacher in Nanyoang public school.

In the meantime, the second great grandmother

suffered two mis-carriages, both boys, before giving birth to my Du-Diaa. In a household of doting grandmother and two mothers, Du-Diaa was loved and overly protected because of his poor health as a baby with chronic stomach problems. He was physically weak; hence, he was kept from other children. If the neighbor children tried to bully or scare Du-Diaa in any way, they would be scolded or punished by the maids as an effort to keep Du-Diaa safe.

Since great grandfather was educated in traditional Chinese as well as abroad, he was moved to work in the Ministry of Foreign Affairs in Beijing. He was responsible for documenting and editing the history for ten years. The family gained prosperity in those years and Du-Diaa described those days as happy and worry free.

On July 28, 1920, Du-Diaa recalled his father was off duty. He was so excited to spend alone time with his father. They went to the Dongan Bazaar and bought new stationary and other articles. They returned at noon.

"I am going to auntie's for lunch and play some mahjong, do you want to come?" Du-Maa asked my great grandfather. She was getting ready to go out in her elegant summer silk qipao.

"Who wants to make companion with you women." Great grand-father responded light heartily. "It is more comfortable to stay home with my son." He said with a chuckle and glanced at Du-Diaa with a knowing smile implying that the father and son will hang out without the interference of hovering females around the house. But he looked unwell. Great grandfather died unexpectedly that evening. Du-Diaa was only nine years old.

Despite the fact that Du-Diaa grew up in a happy and loving family in early childhood, I attributed his poor physical and mental health to the intergenerational trauma of the Chang ancestors, unresolved ACEs of his biological mother, and the trauma of losing his father at such a young age. As the only one son, he had to shoulder the burden of the family according to the old Chinese tradition.

I had very positive memories of Du-Diaa in my childhood. He was the warm adult who treated my sister and me as a typical loving grandfather would. Since my sister was too young, he spent most time with me, taking me to the park, helping me catch tad poles in the lily ponds, telling me Chinese mythical tales, teaching me how to draw, and introducing me to Peking opera.

Du Diaa's family was very concerned about his frail health and timid nature; hence, they prayed to the ancient Kuan Kung warrior, 關公 Guāngōng, and asked the god to be his godfather as a spiritual guardian. Kuan Kung was a warrior of the Han dynasty during the era of the Three Kingdoms. Kuan Kung was known for his strength, courage, and skills on the battle fields. His status of immortality in the Chinese culture was attributed to his dignified character- loyalty, dedication, wisdom, and leadership. Despite his fierce image and ruthless battle skills, Kuan Kung was remembered as the defender of peace for the Chinese people. He gained an immortal status over time and is still worshipped in many temples today.

After Du-Diaa's father passed away, I suspect Kuan Kung became a prominent spiritual figure in Du-Diaa's life. Ever since I was a little girl, I remember the excitement of accompanying Du-Diaa to the Peking Opera. I was mesmerized by the actors with elaborately painted faces and vibrant costumes re-telling the story of the Three Kingdoms. The character of Kuan Kung was portrayed with a fierce red face, long black beard, and wearing colorful armor embroidered with dragon heads. He had the deepest thundering voice that I could feel the floor vibrate under my feet. Kuan Kung always carried in his right hand the signature sword named Green Dragon Crescent Blade. Du-Diaa spoke of Kuan Kung as a real godfather. In a child's innocent mind, I actually believed that the Kuan Kung on the stage was an image of one of my real great grandfathers. I also thought my ancestors spoke in sing-songs as in the Peking Opera. I use to imitate the high pitch voice of the female characters of the Peking Opera, prance around on my toes, create dancing mudra with my fingers, and imagine that I was on stage. Du-Diaa would sing along in his Peking Opera throaty voice of Kuan Kung.

We happened to live right next to Fu Hsing School of Peking Opera in Beitou. Now known as the Fu Hsing

Dramatic Arts Academy, or the high school for the performing arts–Fame of Taiwan. It was a boarding school for students starting from age eight to 18. Every morning at the break of dawn, we could hear students warming up their vocal cords, practicing the high pitch voices of the female role or the vigorous voices of the male hero characters for the vocal class. Du-Diaa knew the principal of the academy, who lived on campus with his family, hence, we visited the school often for afternoon tea. I enjoyed watching the students practicing the combat scenes with extraordinary acrobatic skills in synchrony with the fast bamboo drum beats. I cringed when I saw the younger students straddled against the wall with force to increase their flexibility. They never uttered a sound, but you could see the tears streaming down their faces as they endured the excruciating pain. All the discipline and rigorous training always came together in gorgeous performances of fanatical precision splendor that I remember vividly.

Many pleasant childhood memories with Du-Diaa often include foggy vignettes of me as a ten or eleven-year old child, guiding a drunken adult home late at night. For some reason, I cannot re-call how we got home, but we always did. I learned to be the "responsible one" at a very young age. Du-Diaa's decades of unreciprocated love for my grandmother often turned into romantic poems and short stories. Many of his stories were published in journals and newspapers. He enjoyed practicing Chinese brush painting for leisure. In addition to Peking Opera characters, he loved to paint birds. I vividly remember the eyes of his painted birds as sad and lifeless. For some reason unknown to me at the time, my father did not respect his father, in fact he detested Du-Diaa. The family labeled Du-Diaa as a "spineless" weak man who was fearful of his wife. As a child, I remember Du-Diaa would be tearful and sad when he was drunk, but he was always kind and gentle towards me and my sister. He was the one adult who buffered us from our ACEs and trauma.

Self-Healing Moment

Mindful Inquiry

- Find a quiet and private place.
- Have a pen and journal nearby as an option.
- Sit comfortably.
- Look around you and behind you slowly.
- Notice three objects in your space; name two sounds you hear; name one feeling.
- Feel the ground with your feet, and the seat supporting you.
- Take three deep breaths.
- Ask yourself the following questions:
  o Can you re-call a generational trauma experienced by your ancestors?
  o When were your ancestors experienced the trauma? What were the circumstances?
  o How did that story pass down to you?
  o How did your body respond to these questions?
  o Give yourself a loving hug before RAIN practice:
- **Recognize** any sensations in your body.
- **Allow** it to be there with loving kindness.
- **Investigate** the sensation with curiosity.
- **Nurture** your body with compassion and comforting touch.

- Breathe deeply.
- Notice if there is anything else lingering that no longer serve you.
- Shake your body or dance.
- Optional: write down your experience in a journal.

8 MY ACES

∞ ♥ ∞

"Watch your thoughts, they become your words; watch your words, they become your actions;

watch your actions, they become your habits; watch your habits, they become your character; watch your character, it becomes your destiny."

-Lao Tzu

After my mother left, my childhood froze. I turned from a talkative smart little girl to a silent child with learning disabilities and behavioral problems. Ironically, I started kindergarten one year early, because I was considered a very inquisitive gifted child with big vocabularies. I quickly became a "dumb kid" in school.

"Look at 張錦蕾 Zhāng-jǐn-lěi," I recall a teacher called me out in class.

"Doesn't she look so serious as if she is paying attention in class? But you have no idea what she is thinking or where her mind wandered to." I remember just staring at the teacher blankly, but secretly thinking, what is wrong with me? My brain seemed to stop functioning after my mother left me at first grade. I could not grasp math, memorize the multiplication table, or remember homework assignments. I failed most of the tests. I felt like I was walking in a thick fog and looking for a way out, but can't. In the summers, the cicadas in the school banyan trees would hum in unison. I often find myself drawn to the deep numbing hums until I disappear. I went through grade school with the humming cadence of the cicadas.

I went to Wego Elementary school of Beitou. Ironically, it was a Christian missionary sponsored orphanage with a private school opened for commuter students like me. My mother selected that school, because of its English curriculum. She knew I will be an American one day. Most of my friends were orphans, I often felt like I was one of them. I remembered sharing my bento with my orphan girl class mates after school, because they craved for delicious home cooking instead of the typical cafeteria food. Although my sisters and I were often neglected emotionally living without parents, we were well taken care of with food and shelter.

Drawing and painting kept me in my own safe bubble. I would create picture stories and disappear for hours in the imaginary world that I painted on paper. I loved The Little Mermaid by Hans Christian Anderson. I was drawn to the magical world under water and the tragic ending of The Little Mermaid. My story book would be filled with sea creatures, gigantic oysters with pearls, and pretty mermaids swimming around the sea forest. I would immerse myself under the sea, protected by the storm on the ocean surface, and I enveloped myself in silence for hours. I would create characters from mythical stories that I had seen from the Chinese Operas. As I sat alone and looked into the space wondering what to draw next, adults would often comment that "Betsy is day dreaming again." Finally, Ching-Ma would send me to brush painting school over the summers to keep me out of trouble.

In Chinese culture, food was a common thread of comfort. We are very much a foodie family to this day. I am very grateful that we were blessed with the comfort of foods growing up. The memory of family dinner was like soothing balm to the roughness of living in a house of coldness. I remember we had a cook, named Law-Liu. He was a retired soldier from the Nationalist Party. In my mind's eyes, I can still see his leathery face with big grins that revealed his yellow buck teeth. He always smelled like fresh garlics. He had a very kind heart. He fondly called me

小姐 Xiǎo-jiě, little mistress. Every morning before school, he would prepare warm porridge, salted egg, and soy-pickled radish as breakfast for me. After breakfast, he walked me to school. For lunch, he would prepare bento (a rectangular tin box) with rice, red-braised pork belly and vegetables, such as winter green stir-fry. The tin bento was always tied neatly with hemp string, a woodened tag with my name. Before class, the commuter students would drop off the bentos in the steamer room at the school cafeteria. The big steamer would always be piled-up high with colorful bento boxes. When the school bell rang for lunch, the students lined up in a swift orderly manner. The orphans in one line heading to the cafeteria, and the commuter students in another, lined up to fetch our personal bento from the steam room. I remember the orphan students would always look enviously to the commuter students wondering what was in each bento.

After my mother left, Law-Liu would pick me up after school. I looked forward to coming home to a comforting afternoon snack, such as green bean pudding, sweet potato soup, hot steamed bun with sweet red bean paste, or ripe tomato sprinkled with lots of sugar. Dinner was a family affair and a stable anchoring event of my childhood. In hindsight, family dinner time was a dose of normalcy growing up, despite the undercurrent of dysfunctional relationships within the Chang family. Our typical dinner, always included delicious Shanghainese cuisine such as savory winter melon in bone broth, with four to five dishes of braised meat, seafood, mixed vegetable, etc. After dinner, we had seasoned fresh fruits. In the summer, chilled watermelon was our favorite. Interesting that one of my favorite pass times after dinner, was sitting on granduncle's lap, and he would read to me the comics page of the daily newspaper. On weekend, preparing lunch together with my aunts was one of the highlights. From a very young age, my aunts taught me how to wrap Shanghai big won-tons with pork and Shepherd's purse filling, and fold dumplings with pleats at the edges. As a little girl, I could eat ten dumplings easily in one sitting. New Year's Eve dinner was most meaningful. Ching-Ma would plan the menu and delegate the servants to buy fresh produce, chicken and meat at the Beitau open market. I remember Law-Liu would start preparing the feast many days ahead. Every dish had a special meaning. He started with golden egg dumplings that symbolized wealth and prosperity. Instead of the flour wraps, the dumplings were wrapped in thin miniature egg omelets that he had to create on a small metal pan one at a time. I use to watch him for hours, as the edges of each miniature omelet curled up, he would drop a spoonful of the meat fillings in the center, then seal each omelets perfectly. The half-moon shaped egg dumpling represented the traditional currency of gold ingots in old China. We would have hot pot with tripe, pheasant eggs, and young bamboo shoots, these key ingredients symbolically represent bountiful sons and grandsons. The preparation would continue as the lady housekeeper, Ai-Shung, scrubbed the floor and washed the windows in preparation for the New Year celebration.

New Year celebration lasted weeks, filled with family visits, sweets treats, and red envelopes with crisp new dollars. After the New Year's Eve dinner, the first day of New Year, always started with the fried sweet sticky rice pancake, symbolically representing family sticking together and living a sweet life. Lunch we would have stir-fried sticky rice cake with pork slivers, shitake mushroom and chives, follow by afternoon snack of more sweet rice wine and rice ball soup. Despite my unusual circumstances, New Year celebrations were always fun for children. I learned not to miss having my own parents around, as we were surrounded by extended families and relatives.

Ching-Ma enjoyed entertaining guests. She was a wonderful hostess. Her dinner parties were opportunities to show case her three beautiful daughters to potential suiters. Ching-Ma was the Chinese version of the Mrs. March in the Louisa May Alcott's book Little Women, always looking for a suitable match for her daughter. As I mentioned, the Chang family looked up to the European and American culture. Naturally, people with white-bodies were considered superior. Hence Ching-Ma liked to invite "important" guests including many Caucasians to our dinner parties. For example, our guests frequently included people like the Catholic priests and missionaries from various churches in Beitou, officials in the city government, and businessmen trading with American companies. Ching-Ma had a very different personality at these events, she was out-going, talkative, and smiled a lot. She would be in her best silk gipao dress cover by a perfectly pressed traditional Japanese embroidered apron. She was well known in town for her delicious Western cuisine. We had a rare commodity that most household would envy, a portable American oven. Ching-Ma's specialty was oven roasted chicken, and my Aunt would bake buttery European cake as dessert. All the guests raved about Ching-Ma's special potato salad made with cubes of cucumbers, carrots, peas, and crispy chunks of apples mixed in with rich mayonnaise from America. In the 1960's, apples did not naturally grow in the tropical climate of Taiwan, hence apples were considered a precious fruit reserved for special dinners. My sister and I were often part of these fancy dinner parties, we were well behaved as expected. We were well taught to be seen and not heard as good little children. Whenever Ching-Ma smiled, the tensions around the household melted away. Those days seemed magical looking back. I hung onto those moments whenever I felt sad.

I was in the first grade before my mother left. Occasionally, she would surprise me by taking time off from work and pick me up after school. I remember the sheer delight of spotting my mother outside the class room waiting among the other parents under the banyan tree. She always looked stylish in her short permed hair, dark sun glasses, and wearing American fashion of the 1960's era that set her apart from other moms. And, my mother, a traditional Chinese wife, never learned how to cook!

Self-Healing Moment

Mindful Savoring

- Pick a favorite piece of fruit, a nut, a raisin, a chocolate candy, or any small piece of savory food you choose.
- Find a quiet place without distraction.
- Place the food in your mouth with the intention to enjoy.
- Mindfully and slowly chewing, tasting, and feeling the texture the food with your tongue.
- Notice any sensation, memory, or thoughts evoked by the sense of taste.
- Simply notice with acceptance and contentment.

9 INTERSECTIONALITY

∞ ♥ ∞

"Intersectionality forces people to interact with, listen to, and consider people they don't usually interact with, listen to, or consider."

-Ijeoma Oluo, So you want to talk about race

1963 was a significant year of the civil rights movement filled with the most tragic events of the US history. Elsie arrived in Honolulu, USA in January of 1963, before the famous "I Have a Dream" speech by Dr. Martin

Luther King Jr. and the assassination of President Kennedy. She re-called a box of Kleenex was only twenty five cents at the time. Arriving on the US soil and smelling the plumeria scented air of Hawaii, my mother told me that she felt like "a fish found water." She was finally freed from the oppressive culture that she left behind. As soon as she arrived, she got a job with Aloha Motor in the Human Resources department, and enjoyed the freedoms of an independent working American woman. Hawaii was a culturally diverse island and Elsie fit right in. She was very much isolated from the unprecedented numbers of civil rights demonstrations sweeping the US mainland in the first half of 1963.

My mother's second husband, I will refer to him as Mr. T, was eighteen years older than her. According to my mother, he was a kind man. Their marriage was based on mutual benefits and was never based on love. My mother always said she was grateful for marrying Mr. T. Their marriage paved a pathway for Elsie's parents and siblings eventually immigrating to the US and becoming citizens. It was impossible to immigrate directly to the US for Chinese living in Taiwan at that time. Elsie became an US citizen three years later. In 1965, she returned to Taiwan and gave birth to another daughter. My maternal grandmother took care of her and the newborn. I re-call vaguely that she visited us before giving birth. We were never close to our half-sister growing up.

Elsie never really raised her children by herself in Taiwan. She always had a full time office job and hired a nanny who took care of me and my sister. Interestingly, her second husband gave her an allowance of $240 a month and persuaded her to stay home to raise their daughter. Later, Elsie shared that although many mothers enjoyed the luxury of staying home during the formative years of their young children, she was not happy staying home during those three year with her young child as a house wife. She felt disconnected socially and financial uncomfortable with the dependency on her husband. As soon as her daughter turned three years old, Elsie returned to the workforce as a bank teller in Honolulu. My mother was a fast learner and excelled at the work place. She was promoted to manage the new general leger information system and was given the responsibility to generate the monthly reports. She proudly shared with me that she received recognition as the Most Valuable Employee of the bank.

∞ ♥ ∞

During the years separated from my mother, she would take vacation time from work to visit us once a year in Taiwan. I remember the intense joy of seeing her and the excruciating pain of her leaving again a few days later. She was very much disconnected as a mother to us, but my sister and I craved the loving embrace and the happy moments we shared in those days. I remember one year during my mother's visit, she was appalled to find my long black hair infested with lice. She took me to a hair salon and instructed the hair dresser to cut my hair into a short bob. I did not say a word as tears rolled down my face, and watched the lady chop off my long hair. But inside my gut, I was devastated and angry. I was too young to understand that it was necessary to get rid of the head lice. All I felt was that my mother did not know me at all, because I always wanted to have long hair. I disliked the mandated short hair cut at the ear level of the local public school girls. I felt pretty in my long hair even with lice.

"Why were you not here to keep me clean and free of lice?" I heard myself screaming inside.

"Why didn't you tell me? I did not know you liked long hair?" To this day she is still puzzled by my intense silent reaction of that incident.

How could I disobey and displease my mother, when I treasure each moment of seeing her? She flew in like a whirl wind, we had a few fun days, then she was gone! My mother knew nothing about the life of my sister and I growing up in a household as unwanted children and unprotected. I did not know that in exchange for my mother to see us briefly in those years, she had to send money to pay for additional expenses for us per Ching-Ma's demand. In between visits, she would ship packages of pretty dresses from America. Ching-Ma would dress my sister and me in these pretty dresses, and bring us to a local photography studio for our annual photoshoot that she sent to me parents abroad as proof that we were well cared for.

∞ ♥ ∞

Elsie always expressed her deep gratitude for the

opportunity of becoming an American citizen. The Asian American experience of her generation was different, because they came to this country by choice with hope of a better future. Her Western education and fluency in English prepared her to thrive in America. Once Elsie became a US citizen, she was able to sponsor her parents and all her siblings to Hawaii. Later many of them moved to California. The Paper Tiger's family established new roots in America, land of hope and abundance. The old wealth of the Paper Tiger no longer existed, but the pride of the family legacy and the siblings' closeness provided a virtual anchor of resilience in the new land.

Later my mother with her second husband and young daughter moved to San Francisco. I was delighted to hear the news from her letter. By that time, my sister and I already joined my father and was living with his new family on the East coast. I secretly dreamt that perhaps mother and daughters will be re-united again. In 1971, San Francisco Unified School District (SFUSD) was ending a century of school segregation from 1851 to 1971. The beautiful city fondly named by the Chinese as the Old Golden Mountain was polarized with heated discussions about school desegregation. They arrived in the city in the midst of public protest about bussing and civil unrest. Let me pause here to provide some historical context.

∞ ♥ ∞

In 1851, when the first public schools opened in San Francisco, it was only for the white students. Hence the first segregated public school for black children opened in 1854, the first segregated public school for Chinese children opened in 1859. In 1860 California Education Code explicitly prohibited Black, Asian, and American Indian students from attending the public school with white students. Hence racially segregated schools were formed in the Black Indigenous Persons of Color (BIPOC) communities. Interestingly, in 1870, SFUSD closed the segregated Chinese school only, and barred Chinese American students from attending the white public schools. Fifteen years later, Chinese American community activism led to the California's Supreme Court decision to give the Chinese students the rights to attend public schools. As an effort to avoid school integration, SFUSD finally allowed the segregated school to re-open. As more Asian American Pacific Islanders, such as Japanese and

Korean, immigrated to San Francisco, they were assigned to the Chinese Schools, as another tactic to defer school integration.

∞ ♥ ∞

Although my mother loved the cosmopolitan city life and the freedom of taking trollies to work and shopping independently, her husband was troubled by the anti-Chinese sentiments and concerns for his daughter's safety going to public school in San Francisco. They moved back to Hawaii. Indirectly, racism and Asian hate, shattered my dream and further separated me and my sister from our birth mother.

My mother worked for her brother's jewelry store upon her return to Hawaii. But she felt like a caged bird on the small island, she was not happy, after all she was a city girl. Her second husband had a traditional expectation of a wife's role, and their marriage started to fracture. This time, she stayed in the loveless marriage until her young daughter turned seventeen and left the island for college on the mainland. When my mother became an empty nester at the age of fifty, she divorced her second husband and moved to California. By that time I was a grown woman living in Los Angeles and working as a registered nurse. My mother stayed with me in my small one-bed room apartment for a short time. She had no problem finding a job with another bank and rent her own apartment. Elsie was always quick to land back on her two feet, a strength that I also inherited. As much as I was delighted to be close to my mother again, our relationship had evolved. We were more like good friends than mother and daughter. I remember her favorite song at that time was Bobby McFerrin's "Don't Worry Be Happy". Our favorite pass time was shopping together. I admired her resilience, and the ability to move on to find her own happiness. She was present at the birth of my first daughter. I am glad that at least my daughters had the opportunity to know their grandmother.

Self-Healing Moment

Metta (Loving-Kindness) Practice

- Sit up tall.
- Place both feet on the ground.
- Place both hands palms down on your lap, feel the connection between your palms resting on your thighs.
- Before you close your eyes, look around your space.
- Cognitively register where you are right now, perhaps notice one thing you did not notice before.
- Give yourself the permission to Be Here Now.

Check in

- Notice how you are feeling at this moment, find a word to describe it.
- Take few cleansing breaths.
- Deep breath in through the nose, open your mouth, and sigh out with an Ah (feel free to make a loud ahhh sound).
- Repeat until you feel a sense of letting go and your body softens.

- If it feels good, shake your arms and stump your feet, and shake out anything that do not serve you right now.
- Find some stillness.

Anchoring

- Notice the quietness.
- Bring your awareness to your feet, find a sense of grounding, a sense of rooting down.
- Imaging that you are a tree with roots connecting with the earth beneath you, drawing up energy up through your calves.
- Feel the connection of your thighs with your seat, fully supported by the chair you are sitting on.
- Lengthen your torso from the base of your spine towards the crown of your head.
- Row your shoulders up, back and down, a few times, release your shoulder blades down your back.
- Imaging a plumb line from you ear lobe, shoulder, elbow and hip.
- Soften your face.
- Unclench your jaw.

Breath Awareness

- Bring your awareness to your breath, simply observe without changing it.

- Inhale - notice the cool air entering your nostrils, expanding rib cage and belly.
- Exhale - notice belly and rib cages drawing in, and a slightly warmer air exiting the nostrils.
- Find the breaths cycle and rhythm that feels at ease.
- If focusing on your breath is uncomfortable, feel free to place one hand on your belly, focus on the rise and fall off your belly with each breath cycle.
- Use your breath as an anchor to stay in the present moment.

Loving-Kindness Practice

- Bring both hands to your heart center.
- Take a deep breath in and a slow smooth breath out.
- Bring to your mind's eye someone you adore, could be your love one, or a pet.
- Imagine the person or pet in front of you.
- Say the Metta Mantra to the person you adore with each breath cycle.
  - May you be well & happy.
  - May you be healthy & strong.
  - May you be safe & protected.
  - May you be peaceful & at-ease.
- Take a deep breath in and a slow smooth breath out.

- Bring to your mind's eye, the image of your best self at any age.
- See your best self in front of you with your mind's eye.
- Repeat the Metta Mantra to yourself with each breath cycle.
    o May I be well & happy.
    o May I be healthy & strong.
    o May I be safe & protected.
    o May I be peaceful & at-ease.
- Take a deep breath in and a slow smooth breath out.
- Bring to your mind's eye, someone neutral, perhaps a friend or a co-worker.
- See the person in front of you with your mind's eye.
- Say the Metta Mantra to the person with each breath cycle.
    o May you be well & happy.
    o May you be healthy & strong.
    o May you be safe & protected.
    o May you be peaceful & at-ease.
- Take a deep breath in and a slow smooth breath out.
- Go back to your breath, inhale deeply and exhale slowly and smoothly.
- Continue your normal breathing.
- That is Metta…Loving Kindness.

10 SECRETS

∞ ♥ ∞

"As long as you keep secrets and suppress information, you are fundamentally at war with yourself [. . .]. The critical issue is allowing yourself to know what you know. That takes an enormous amount of courage."

-Bessel Van der Kolk, The Body Keeps the Score

Based on a scientific study, children who grow up with adverse childhood experiences tend to have greater resiliency if they had one or more supporting adults. In addition to Du-Diaa, I had three aunts who were kind to my sister and me. Aunt Peggy was the younger sister of my father and the oldest daughter of the three aunts. She was pretty, sociable, outgoing, and popular. She was the most independent and rebellious of the three aunts. I remember her having a closet full of fancy dresses with shoes made with matching fabric. I loved to sneak into her room and try on her high heels as a kid. She even competed as Miss Taiwan, but she did not win the title because she was not tall enough. Ching-Ma never approved of her boyfriends; hence, I was always assigned as the "chaperone" on her dates. I was only eight years old! Acting as the chaperone on their dates became my permanent role growing up with my aunts. As I mentioned earlier, I was groomed to be a little grown up at a very young age. It foreshadowed my role in the future. Eventually, Aunt Peggy was forbidden to marry her boyfriend, who was a singer and entertainer, a profession not acceptable in the traditional Chinese family. Instead, Aunt Peggy married a tall, handsome white Australian, who worked in the finance sector. They were introduced through the family's foreign relations. I remember their grand wedding was the show of the town. The wedding was held at the Grand Hilton Hotel of Taipei. The newlyweds were interviewed on National TV because they were considered the first interracial marriage between Taiwan and Australia. Instead of including the bride's only nieces in the wedding party, perhaps as flower girls, Ching-Ma hired two cute little kids, total strangers, to be the flower girl and ring bearer because they looked the part in the perfectly orchestrated wedding photos. Judy and I sat with our household servants instead of family at the wedding. We were just girls with no value to Ching-Ma at such an important event.

Aunt Bell, in the middle, was the quiet and obedient one. She was Ching-Ma's favorite daughter because Aunt Bell was betrothed to a young man from a wealthy Chinese family who was studying abroad at the Columbia University Doctorate Program in the US. This marriage was arranged by my Great Aunt Sally while Aunt Bell was still in high school. My Great Aunt Sally was Ching-Ma's younger sister, who married a rich man in America. Great Aunt Sally had an important role in the Chang family because she provided some financial support to Ching-Ma. Also Du-Diaa worked for the China Shipping Company owned by Great Aunt Sally's former husband. I remember that as a child, every birthday I would receive a pretty birthday card from the US signed "Sally" by this infamous Great Aunt Sally. I heard she was the most beautiful daughter of the King family and married well. Before I was born, Ching-Ma would leave Du-Diaa and family behind to accompany Great Aunt Sally on luxurious vacations in Japan. They were well connected in the high society in Tokyo. I learned that Ching-Ma met a professor from the University of Taiwan Medical School on that trip. They continued their love affair openly after she returned from Japan. Per my aunt, my grandmother was gone months and sometimes a full year. During that time, Du-Diaa would be depressed and get drunk every night.

Aunt Pauline, the youngest, was the closest to me

because she was only fifteen when I was born. She treated me like a little sister. She was also the most academic one among the three aunts. Hence, she was the one who tutored me and forced me to memorize the multiplication table. I remember hiding from her, so I did not have to recite the multiplication table that I struggled to learn. Today, I would be identified as a problem child with a cognitive learning disability. I was also the designated chaperone on all her dates when I was about ten years old.

∞ ♥ ∞

Without the help of my aunts, I would not have completed grade school. For example, one summer vacation, I neglected to complete all school assignments. The day before school started, my three aunts all pitched in to help me complete the assignments, including pages of calligraphy. I suspect the teacher knew, because a second grader could not have completed pages of Chinese calligraphy with such neatness. I had a lot of anxiety going to school because I knew I was failing. My brain could not absorb any knowledge. I would often run away on the day of exams. I remember during the third grade on a cloudy day after Law-Liu, our cook, dropped me off to school, I ditched school. My mother used to bring me to Tian-Mu, a town over twenty miles away, to visit her parents. It was a distance of at least thirty to forty minutes by car. I walked in my rubber rain boots for four hours hoping to find my mother. By some miracle I knew how to get to my maternal grandparents' house on foot. My grandmother was home and was shocked to see me. After feeding me lunch, my uncle put me on his motorcycle and brought me right back to school. I was so disappointed for not finding my mother and my grandmother did not offer to take me in. I remember all of the teachers and students staring at me as I rode back to school on the loud motorcycle. I received a spanking on my left palm at the principal's office. Ching-Ma was livid. I do not remember what happened after the scolding. I stopped running away to seek relative's protection after that incident. Sadly, I realized my maternal grandmother did not welcome me either. I learned to escape into my imaginary world instead, and I would quietly slip back into the physical reality without any adults discovering what I did to avoid more punishment. It was magic.

Growing up in Taiwan, corporal punishment and spanking were the norm at school and at home. There is fine line between physical neglect and abuse of children. Hitting children was the acceptable cultural norm. Hence, I had difficulty doing my own ACE screening. I did not consider myself sexually abused because I cannot remember recurrent abuse. But, in hindsight my upbringing was not normal based on what I can remember. What I remember as "games" with adults were incidences of child molestation based on the definitions I learned as an adult.

I lived in a very dysfunctional arrangement but I

always thought it was normal. We lived in a big home with two separate dwellings and a big courtyard in the middle. The lower main house had two bedrooms adjacent to each other, where Ching-Ma and my grand-uncle lived. The house was decorated in European style, with a large living room and dining area where the family gathered for meals and entertained guests. The upper dwelling was decorated in traditional Japanese style, which was very common in Taiwan due to former Japanese occupation. It had a family room and sleeping quarters with a separate family room and a study. Each house had its own bathrooms. The houses were divided by a courtyard shaded by bamboo trellises covered in grapevines. Ching-Ma would make homemade sweet wine from the annual grape harvest. A pathway lined with jasmine flowers connected the two houses. In the summer, the garden was filled with the scent of jasmine, as my sister and I played in the courtyard, cooling off after the humid summer day. In the winter, the jasmine went dormant and the bright red poinsettias bloomed along the two side walls of the courtyard. The picturesque courtyard was a frequent back drop for our family photos.

After my father left, my mother moved in with her in-laws. Three of us shared a room in the upper house. After my mother left, Ching-Ma changed the sleeping arrangement. My sister shared a bedroom with Du-Diaa in the upper house. Ching-Ma moved me to the main house with her and grand-uncle, who was actually Ching-Ma's boyfriend and lover. I slept in his room. I started experience chronic bed wetting sleeping in that room. I learned about this family secret that everybody seemed to know and accept as normal. Grand-uncle was part of the Cao family, the household that saved Du-Diaa's ancestors, Grand-Uncle Cao was consider the most important person of the Chang household at the time. Hence Du-Diaa had to bow down and allow such outrageous arrangements per his wife's demand. As an adult, I finally understood how much my father despised his own father for allowing such an arrangement. Under the pretense of honoring ancestral obligation, Ching-Ma's "open marriage" only caused humiliation and shame to my father and my aunts. I now understood the toxic source of the mental health and physical health issues that my father and aunts had in later years. I carry the deep shame in my body as well.

Many buried childhood memories revealed itself, as missing pieces of a jigsaw puzzle, during the process of writing this book. I am learning to shed the habitual self-blaming thought of "what is wrong with you?" and accepting what happened to me with self-compassion. Under the Japanese occupation and influence, Beitau had many charming hidden Ryokan, a type of traditional Japanese inn that feature tatami-matted rooms as well as private and communal hot mineral baths called Onsen. Grand-uncle frequently brought me to Ryokans for overnight stays. Sometimes Ching-Ma would join us. He would often wash me meticulously and tenderly in the private Onsen. I vaguely remember the comforting sensation of the warm mineral spring water cascading from the wooden bucket down my little naked body. I always felt very sleepy after the warm bath. I vaguely remember being carried to the tatami bed and being tucked in the cozy futon. Grand-uncle would caress me and kiss me on the lips. I remember feeling his tongue like a fat worm in my mouth and being bewildered. I would be overcome with drowsiness and disappear into a deep warm fog. I was a living doll, a play thing, for Ching-Ma's lover for several years after my mother left. Once my Aunt Bell immigrated to the US to get married, I do not know who made the decision, but I was finally moved to the other house and shared a room with my youngest aunt. My bed wetting habit stopped.

I like to believe that the childhood neglect and abuse I experienced were unintentional. But detrimental adult actions, are often misinterpreted as harmless and love by young children, and are extremely toxic and damaging to our soul-bodies. Since we were kept in separate houses, I do not know my sister's experience, other than the physical beatings she experienced. She always thought I was more favored by Ching-Ma because I had fewer beatings. Regardless, we were both harmed deeply as young children because girls were not valued.

∞ ♥ ∞

I am grateful that now I have trauma-informed resources to purge the pus out of the wound and process the clean pain that I need to experience in order to heal. Recently, I shared the odd sleeping arrangement part of the story with my mother on our weekly calls. She was appalled and sadden. But again, she had no idea our grandmother would do such harm to her own grandchildren. My mother was glad that both my sister and I did not attend Ching-Ma's funeral. But I think our childhood abuse was too much for my mother to process as a grandmother in her eighties.

Today I have over twenty-five stitches combined on my body due to many different childhood "accidents." Some I remember vividly, some vaguely, but I have the scars to prove that something awful happened. I don't know how many scars or stitches are on my soul-body.

In fifth grade, I started to gain weight. I only recall that all of my uniforms became too tight on me. People would tease me about getting fat. But I was not eating. I actually lost my appetite. I was not eating my lunch at school and was skipping dinners. I started to experience increasing flank pain. At that time all of my aunts had immigrated abroad, and Ching-Ma was in the US helping her favorite daughter, my Aunt Bell, after giving birth to her first child. Du-Diaa was in charge. Ai-Shung, our morning housekeeper, was asked to come in the afternoon to take care of my sister and me after school. No one realize that I was seriously ill until a family friend noticed and recommended Du-Diaa take me to see a doctor. I was diagnosed with pediatric kidney disease and hospitalized for a few days. Later I was sent home to rest with restricted activities. The cause of the kidney disease was unknown, but it was serious enough that the doctor ordered me to withdraw from school for one year of treatment and frequent lab tests. I was prescribed a no salt diet. Di-Diaa had no idea how to take care of a child, let alone a sick one. Ai-Shung was not educated. They figured that if I could not eat salty food, the only option was to feed me cake and pastries. As a kid, I did not mind eating cake and pastries every day for a year. It was a miracle that I did not develop other conditions such as diabetes. I started my period while I was ill. One day, I discovered my lower body covered with blood, my underwear soaked. I screamed and thought for sure I was going to die. Luckily Ai-Shung was there to help me. I recovered from my kidney disease after one year of rest. When Ching-Ma came back from the US with another infant granddaughter in her arms, I was ready to go back to school. No one informed my parents of my serious illness.

I had to repeat the fifth grade, but the serious illness had changed me. Miraculously, I came back to my body and was able to focus on school again. My teachers jokingly said my illness made me a better student. I finally realized that my destiny was in my own hands - I wanted to live. Ching-Ma had a new granddaughter whose parents would send money to support every month. As my sister and I became older, we were harder to control. Hence, it was time to send us to join my father in the US. After sixth grade, my father and mother both separately paid Ching-

Ma tuition to send us to the English language immersion at the American school. Ching-Ma pocketed half of the tuition and only sent me to American school and not my sister, Judy.

∞ ♥ ∞

In the summer of 1970, Ching-Maa put my sister and me on an airplane headed to Baltimore, Maryland via Hawaii. I remember vividly the strong aroma of the unfamiliar scent of coffee that made us so sick we threw up on the airplane. The flight attendants were all very friendly to us. Seeing two little "oriental girls" traveling alone, the other passengers would try to start conversations with us. Although the term "Asian American" is the academic term originating from the University of California at Berkley in 1968, people like me from Eastern ancestral origins were still commonly identified by the term "oriental" through the early 1970's as part of the Western process of racializing Asians as forever the "other." We would respond in very broken English and smile. My sister and I were elated to be able to see our mother again. We had a layover in Honolulu for a few days. We had to stay at my maternal uncle's house because my mother's husband would not allow us to be in their home. My mother visited us, and we finally met the Paper Tiger's other grandchildren, cousins whom we had not met for over a decade or meeting for the first time. We did not realize at the time that the rest of the US was not like Hawaii at all. My mother bought us many pretty outfits, including a beautiful traditional Hawaiian mu-mu, and put us on the airplane to mainland. The flight to Baltimore Maryland was long. This time my sister and I were consumed with the sadness of leaving our mother again. We both sobbed uncontrollably for the entire trip until we landed at Baltimore-Washington Airport.

Self-Healing Moment

Yoga Asana for Grief

- Find a quiet and private place with a soft carpeted floor or use a yoga mat or your bed.
- Practice Child's Pose (Balasana) – a healing pose for when you are feeling sad and your body just want to curl in.
- Instructions: Come onto your shins with the top of your feet on the floor or mat.
- Bring your big toes together and spread your knees comfortably apart.
- Shift your hips back towards your heels.
- Reach your arms in front of you and place your hands in a relaxed manner, slightly wider than the width of your shoulders.
- Rest your forehead on the mat or on a soft block to give your mind a rest.
- Breathe normally and let go.
- Be here as long as you wish, allowing your body to feel and emotions to be released.
  (Note: If you have tender knee joints, please roll up a soft blanket or use a pillow behind your knees).

11 THE AMERICAN DREAM

∞ ♥ ∞

"… Raindrops keep falling on my head
But that doesn't mean my eyes will soon be turning red
Crying's not for me
'Cause I'm never gonna stop the rain by complaining
Because I'm free
Nothing's worrying me

… It won't be long till happiness steps up to greet me…"

-B.J. Thomas

Our father picked us up from the Baltimore-Washington International airport with a station wagon, and the radio was blasting a new pop song. B. J. Thomas' "Raindrops Keep Fallin' on My Head" was the first song I heard that forever imprinted in my head associated with my arrival to Baltimore, Maryland. My sister and I felt like foster children dropped into a family of strangers in a foreign land. Historically, Cockeysville, Maryland was the scene of Civil War activities. After the war, the village of Cockeysville was formed along the York Turnpike now known as York Road. It is still considered the countryside before York Road was developed. Our new home on York Road, was a two story old colonial house with a front porch, painted white with winter green shutters. The front of the house was shaded by four tall oak trees. Two acres of grassy back yard extended through a dense field of wild black berry bushes and trees reaching to a small stream. It was a picture perfect American home like nothing we have ever seen growing up in Taiwan.

We met a father whom we had not seen for years, a new Japanese step-mother, a new step-brother, and two new little sisters. Additionally, we had a new Japanese grandmother, who lived in a house next door. My sister and I must have been a sorry sight, both sleep deprived and puffy red eyes from crying.

"You must miss your mother very much…Aww, that is too bad, she doesn't want you anymore…" Japanese Grandmother would say to us between puffs of her cigarette.

"What kind of mother would leave her children? I

would never..." Step-mother would chime in and look at us sideways between puffs of her cigarette. Every adult smoked in that house. That must be the American way.

"You are in America, from now on, you can only speak English in this house. I don't want to hear you speaking Chinese to each other!" The first instruction from my father as we arrived in our new home.

The stench of the cigarette smoke, the little prick of the words in an unfamiliar language started to make me dizzy. The amygdala, little alarm of my primitive brain, started to send signals to my body. "Nothing seems to fit...". My sister and I were exhausted from the long flight and jet lag, so we went to bed and fled into a deep slumber.

We woke up the next day, and received our day one orientation from my step-mother.

"In America, everybody has to work! We do not have servants like you had in Taiwan."

"Betsy, from now on, you are in charge of cleaning downstairs including living room, family room, bathroom and kitchen. Judy, you clean upstairs including all the bedrooms, bathroom, and the attic."

"After dinner, you both can wash the dishes and mop the floor. We will teach you how to use the washing machine later."

Although we were very much neglected living with

Ching-Ma, we never had to do physical labor such as scrubbing the bath room, polish windows, wax the furniture, vacuum the carpets, and mop the floors. In America, we quickly became servant girls. We felt like two Cinderellas.

The American dream quickly turned into a never-ending nightmare, when my sister and I realized that we simply traded the familiar life of unpleasant neglect with occasional punishments, to a new life of daily grind, endless chores, micro-aggression from our step-mother, and domestic violence of a drunken father. By the way, we were also instructed that you can never tell anyone, what happened in the family stayed in the family! Luckily, we had been trained to adapt and survive in our own ways. We were grateful to have each other.

We arrived to the US during summer vacation. My father loved fishing, so he decided to take us on a fishing adventure. We woke up at three in the morning and drove to Chesapeake Bay at dawn. We got on a sports fishing boat with other sports fishermen. He patiently showed us how to set up the fishing poles and the baits. It was our very first fishing experience as father and daughters excursion. We were so delighted to bring home a large ice chest full of striped bass or commonly called "rockfish" by the locals. Then the real work begun, father showed us how to clean the fish from scaling to gutting as he started to get drunk with one too many beers. Judy and I sat on the back porch with newspapers spread out on the floor and cleaned over fifty rock fish as we gagged with the fishy stench. Cleaning fish freshly caught by father became our new chore.

∞ ♥ ∞

Since school had not yet started, the kids were left home alone while our parents worked. We got to know our new siblings. I had no problem with my half-sisters, they were two cute little girls of three and five years old, I was like the new baby sitter. But it was a rough start getting along with my step-brother who was half white and one year younger, we will be in the same grade because I was held back one year due to my illness. We often got into arguments. One time we got into a fist fight, and I got punched so hard in my stomach, I fell over. As I hunched over holding my stomach with shock and in pain, survival instinct kicked in, I realized that I cannot win with a fist fight, he was taller and stronger. Since I am older and technically a stranger in his home, I had to find a way to get along. I offered a truce and tried to be the mature one as girls often were. We became good friends and partners in running the family business in the days to come.

I experienced my first encounter of "racism" before I even knew the meaning of the word. Cockeysville was a very small town in the 1970's. We had very few neighbors in addition to our Japanese grandma living next door. One acre down the hill, a friendly couple lived with their two teenage girls . The husband was a fire fighter, the wife worked in the school administration. Across the fields of apple trees was a single parent family with twelve kids. I learned that the father abandoned them, and the mother had a nervous breakdown. Hence the house hold was managed by the two older girls who were in high school. We often saw all the kids play in the field.

Few weeks after the arrival to my new home, I was sitting on the back porch on a Sunday afternoon, husking freshly purchased corn from the Valley View Farm down the street. I was minding my own business, savoring another new experience, and imaging the silk of the corn as Rapunzel's long hair, when the two boys from the house across the field came over. They were both younger than me, and were looking at me with sheepish grins. I thought they were friendly, so I smiled back. Suddenly the older boy darted over and grabbed my crotch, squeezed hard and ran! I was utterly shocked and speechless. In seconds, they were already half way across the field. Than they turned around with fingers lifting the corners of their eyes.

"Go home, you chink! Ha ha ha…" They ran away laughing.

I never told anyone about the shameful attack, but the word must have spread among the neighbor kids. My step-brother heard about the incidence.

"Don't ever let them do that to you again!" He said to me privately. I suspected he set them straight, the incidence never happened again. But I learned to be on guard and never trust anyone as a new immigrant.

Self-Healing Moment

Choosing Calm

We can always choose where we place our attention; fear and calm are both contagious. So, choose calm.

Grounding

- Sit up straight.
- Place both feet on the floor.
- Place both hands on your lap, feel the back of your chair and the seat beneath you.
- Allow the chair to support you.
- Before you close your eyes, turn your head slowly from side to side, look around your space, cognitively register where you are right now, may be notice one thing you did not notice before …color or texture.

Check in

- Take a moment to notice how you are feeling at this moment, find a word to describe it. When you name it, you release its hold on you.
- Lower your you gaze or close your eyes if you choose.
- Give yourself the permission to be here now.

Body Awareness

- Notice the quietness.

- Bring your awareness to your feet again, find a sense of grounding, a sense of rooting down and connecting with the earth beneath you.
- Feel the connection with your seats and feel the support by the chair you are sitting on.
- Lengthen your torso evenly from the base of your spine towards the crown of your head.
- Maintain the nice long spine.
- Lift your heart and row your shoulders up, back and down, a few times.
- Sit up tall in the full expression of your dignity, while inviting some softness.
- Soften your face.
- Unclench your jaw.

Breath Awareness

- Bring your awareness to your breath... just observe without changing it.
- Notice the cool air entering your nostrils, expanding rib cage and belly, with your inhale.
- Notice your belly and rib cages drawing in, and a slightly warmer air exiting the nostrils with your exhale.
- Notice your energy level...if you feel a hint of anxiousness... notice where you are holding it in your body.
- We can't force our body to relax or release tension, but we can direct our breath to the areas

of our body that are tense, simply invite some softness with each breath.

- Find the breaths cycle and rhythm that feels at ease.

Mind Awareness

- Mindfulness is about focusing on the present moment, with full acceptance, with no judgement or attachment; we have been using our breaths as the focus.

- In yoga, sometimes we use mantra as a repetitive focus, to help engage the mind, and offer a means of getting closer to the stillness within.

- The mantra I am offering today is a simple phrase - "I am Calm."

- Repeat silently to yourself as you Inhale--- I am…

- Calm…as you exhale.

- Inhale- I am.

- Exhale- Calm.

- Feel free to draw out Calm as long as your out-breath permits effortlessly.

- Continue the practice until you experience calm within your body.

12 INITIATION TO ACCULTURATION

∞ ♥ ∞

" Your living is determined not

so much by what life brings to you

as by the attitude you bring to life;

not so much by what happens to you

as by the way your minds look at what happens. "

-Khaili Gibran

September marked the beginning of a new school year. The night before the first day of middle school was filled with anticipation and excitement. Yet I was very nervous. I would be the first Asian immigrant and person of color entering Cockeysville Middle School with all white students. Before going to bed, I laid out on my bed the pretty mu-mu that my mother bought for me in Hawaii. I wanted to look my best and make a positive first impression.

My step-brother and I walked to the bus stop on a nippy autumn morning. A big yellow bus, filled with chattering middle schoolers, stopped before us. I stepped in as all eyes turned toward me. I felt my palms turned cold, I quickly slipped into the first empty seat, took a deep breath, and wishing I had brought along a sweater.

Cockeysville Middle School opened in 1967 after Baltimore county purchased the property from a farmer for only five dollars! The first day of school was a very positive experience, people were very friendly and seemed to be curious about this new girl. I felt very special, in addition to meeting my home room teacher, I had a dedicated English teacher and a teacher's assistant from the upper grade assigned to me, because I was the first and only ESL (English as a Second Language) student. I went home feeling pretty good after a day of orientating to my new school.

That evening, my step-mother came to my room unexpectedly.

"Did you wear a long mu-mu to school today?" She

asked sternly.

"Yeah…" I wonder how did she know, because we left the house before she was up this morning. Maybe she heard from one of the teachers visiting the beauty salon where she worked, since it was the only one in Cockeysville.

"Don't ever wear that funny looking dress to school again! This is not Hawaii, and nobody dresses like that around here. People are gossiping about you!"

"Okay…" I was puzzled by the severity of her tone for such a small thing. But, I was observing and learning, as I had perfected the survival skill at discerning adult's behaviors and adjusting my own actions accordingly ever since I was a five year old abandoned little girl. I put on my invisible armor and was on guard.

The first few weeks of school, I felt like a celebrity. The seventh grade social studies teacher invited me to speak to all his classes about growing up on the island of Formosa, a name dated back to the 1500's, when the Portuguese sailors sighted the uncharted island and named it "Beautiful island" known as Taiwan today. Considering that I was at a disadvantage academically as an ESL student, I quickly learned to leverage my strength in all my assignments with my art skills. For example, we had to do a project for world history class, I decided to illustrate the diversity of countries and cultures through various traditional costumes. I created posters with colorful drawings of men's and women's traditional costumes and headdresses. I provided detailed descriptions of traditional fabrics, symbolic designs with meanings, and cultural practices for each poster. My social studies teacher loved my project so much that she kept all my posters to show other classes. I also volunteered to design and paint mural's in the school hallways during free periods; and created stage sets for annual school musicals. I accumulated extra credits for biology by dissecting a fetal pig and sketching detailed anatomy layer by layer for the teacher to make into transparencies for the overhead projector as teaching aids. I loved the American school system and the opportunity to be creative. It was so different from the schools in Taiwan where I felt restricted and unsuccessful. I thrived. I made the honor roll and was pleasantly surprised to be recognized with the Best Citizen Award at the end of seventh grade. In the subsequent years, I received several awards for number one placements in art contests, and year end recognition from the arts department for overall accomplishments. The school principle purchased my metal sculpture and displayed it in her office. Middle school in America was my happy place, I felt safe in the classrooms.

Feeling safe was not always the case outside of school. Halloween was right around the corner. My sister and I were so excited to participate in the first trick or treat experience. All five kids made our own costumes. My parents dropped us off at the apartment complex nearby. We were so excited going from door to door and seeing our grocery bags fill up with all kinds of treats. As we walked from one apartment building to another in the dark, we were suddenly hit by grenades of raw eggs one after another. We had no idea where the attack came from and we ran! In the dark, you heard kids' laughing at us and yelling: "Trick or treat smell my feet! Go home Chinks! Go home Japs!" It was not a very pleasant experience. My step-mother picked us up and we were all dripping with raw egg yolks.

∞ ♥ ∞

At home, my sister and I felt like we were walking on egg shells constantly with unpredictable tension between my father and step-mother. They fought frequently over the restaurant business and my father's drinking problem. On the surface, they really tried to create an all American family experience for us as parents, despite their limited capacity to love or be parents. Although we were a very secular family and were never raised with any religious beliefs, we learned to recite grace before dinner like what we saw on TV.

"God is great, God is good; let us thank him for our food, Amen." was our prayer of gratitude as we sat around the dining table before meals. Once a while, my parents would surprise us with impromptu picnics at the Beaver Springs. We would pack up into the station wagon with fried chicken, potato salad, carrot sticks, chips, and soda drinks. Sometimes, our parents would reward us with a bowling night on my father's off day from the restaurant. The bowling night always started with a treat of Big Mac, French fries, and Coke at the local McDonalds. We joined the Beaver Dam Swimming Club in the summer, where we spent many summer vacations when we were still too young to work full time at the restaurant. My parents never really planned any trip, it just happened spontaneously. I suspected these idea popped up under the influence of alcohol. I dreaded the annual family vacation to Ocean City, because we never knew if we would make it home alive. Father would be drunk, and step-mother would be yelling in the car, as all of us stayed silent in the back seats keeping our fingers crossed in a cigarette smoke filled car. We were always feeling scared.

It was not long before I assumed the responsible role of taking care of my younger siblings. I was expected to make sandwiches, pack lunches and make dinners. I remember making my first hamburger, I did not know you must make the raw beef patties larger than the actual size. My first hamburgers turned out to be meat balls. The Japanese grandma was kind enough to show me how to make spaghetti sauce with a few teaspoons of soy sauce as the secret ingredient. I mail-ordered a Betty Crocker recipe cards with my allowance and learned to cook the American way. Pretty soon I was responsible for baking all my little sisters' birthday cakes and roasting the Thanksgiving turkey every year. I would get up early on Sundays to make everyone pancakes.

Life was actually quite fun among us five kids when our parents were out of the house. One of us would stand guard at the window, as soon as our parent's car appeared in our view on York Road, the little one would call out "Mom is home!" We would all quickly tidy up and be still.

∞ ♥ ∞

I learned to adjust to my new life. I became very quiet, obedient, and helpful; hence my step-mother started to like me as her good helper. Whereas my sister Judy was more out spoken and not afraid to speak her mind. She had a very difficult time, because our step-mother hated her. Both Judy and I knew we did not belong, it was a matter of time before we could escape this life. I was the first to flee as the oldest. Later, in adulthood, I learned of Judy's heart wrenching stories and suffering after I left home, including inhumane neglect and cruelty by our step-mother when Judy was gravely ill from a severe asthma attack. She was locked in a room, left to die with no medical treatment. Our father never stepped in to stop the maltreatment of his own biological daughter. Miraculously, Judy survived.

∞ ♥ ∞

Children are very adaptable. But our body keeps the score. I started to gain weight from the all American diet. In addition to increased consumption of whole milk, cheese, and meat, there were all kinds of goodies like hot dogs, sugar frosted cereals, ice cream, donuts, potato chips, and Hostess Twinkies in every lunch bag.

" You're starting to have an Onigiri (rice ball) face. Americans don't like that." One day my step-mother jokingly said to me. The words were like pin pricks, but I just smiled and decided to cut back on sweets and fatty foods. It was not pleasant when Onigiri face became my nick name that both father and step-mother started calling me as a cruel joke.

So I started serious dieting, I cut back on my food intake and counted calories every day. I started riding my bike vigorously for one hour in the morning before going to school. I would chew my steak for a long time and spit it out secretly; I watered down the whole milk with water; and only packed half a sandwich for lunch with no sweets or chips. Baby fat started to come off my adolescent body. But when I looked into the mirror, I still saw an Onigiri face. So I kept on dieting, while I felt pretty good about having more control over myself and I continued to excel in school. My period stopped and I was suffering from anorexia nervosa. My parents started to be concerned as I withered in size, but instead of seeking professional treatment for my conditions, they started to harass and shame me about not eating. In order to placate them, I started eating again, especially in front of my parents. But I figured out a way to induce vomiting after I ate. The power struggle continued as I kept my darkest secret. I continued with the eating disorder alternating between anorexia and bulimia through early adulthood.

Self-Healing Moment

Create Inner Balance with Breath

- Deep breathing is one of body's strongest self-healing tools. It lowers blood pressure, reduce heart rate, decreases stress hormones, increases energy and improves immunity.

Grounding

- Sit up tall.
- Place both feet on the ground and hands on your laps.
- Turn your head slowly from side to side, look around your space, cognitively register where you are right now.

Check in

- Take a moment to Check In - notice how you are feeling, what is the state of your mind today? Find a word to describe in.
- Soften your you gaze or close your eyes if you choose.
- Give yourself the permission to be here now.

Body Awareness

- Notice the how your mind starts to settle down in this quietness.

- Bring your awareness to the bottom of your feet, wiggle your toes, and plant them back down onto the floor.

- Find a sense of grounding, a sense of rooting down and connecting with the earth beneath you.

- Draw the earth energy upward through your legs.

- Feel the connection with the back of the chair supporting you.

- Lengthen your torso evenly from the base of your spine towards the crown of your head.

- Sit up a little taller.

- Lift your heart and row your shoulders up, back and down, a few times.

- Maintain this alert but relaxed position.

- Soften your face.

- Unclench your jaw.

- Invite a gentle smile to your face.

Breath Awareness

- Bring your awareness to your breath… observe without changing it for a few breath cycles.

- Start to scan your body with your breath from the top of your head to the bottom of your feet.

- Notice any sensation... where you are holding stress in your body.
- Direct your breath to parts of your body that might need a little softening.
- Invite some softness and gently letting go, at your own pace.
- We have innate resources to heal ourselves with each breath cycle.
- Inhale for your count of 4 and exhale for 4.
- Continue few more cycles to create a sense of inner balance with your breaths.
- As you breath, notice the slight pulse between your inhale and exhale...
- A place of perfect stillness...Linger there for a moment...than exhale...pulse at the end... letting go.
- Now, we are going to Inhale for a count of 4, pulse at the top for 2, exhale for 6
- Continue 4-2-6 breath for six cycles.
- Continue with your own pace, feel free to stop and return to own normal breathing any time you choose.
- Adding on or stay with this pace if it feels good in your body.
- Let go of counting.
- Go back to your normal breathing pattern.
- Notice your energy level.
- Allow few minutes of silence.

- Slowly bring your awareness back to your feet, the chair you are sitting on, and the space around you in the present.
- Check In again - notice how you are feeling at this moment, perhaps there is a shift, find a word to describe it.
- Notice the collective calm energy around you.
- Note: It is perfectly normal, if you experience some spontaneous release of emotion, sometimes in the physical body, such as warm tears, hiccups or even an urge to sneeze. It is a natural way of your body to dissolve some stress that you have been holding on. Allow it to be released naturally...with no self judgement.

13 WORK WORK-WORK

∞ ♥ ∞

"We are all what we repeatedly do. Excellence then is not an act, but a habit."

-Aristotle

One lesson I quickly learned as a new arrival to America was the work ethic instilled in me by my immigrant parents. Work-work-work! You must always work hard to succeed in life. I was curious and wondered why my father, who never cooked a meal before coming to the US, became a restaurant owner? Why Asian Americans often associated with restaurants and laundry businesses in the US?

It was interesting to learn how historical anti-Chinese policies shaped the choices immigrants made to succeed in the country of hopes and dreams. The early Chinese restaurants in the US started during the California Gold rush, which brought the early wave of Chinese immigrants from the Canton province. Since women were banned from immigrating to the US to join their husbands, restaurants and laundry businesses started as necessities to provide services traditionally done by wives or other females. Although the Chinese Exclusion Act, a Federal Law signed by President Chester A. Author in 1882, prohibited all immigration of Chinese laborers, the act allowed the merchants to enter the country. In 1915, the restaurant owners became eligible for merchant VISA. Hence the Chinese restaurants became another pathway for Chinese immigrants. Today, you will find at least one Chinese restaurant or take out in every city of the US. As an effort to make Chinese food palatable for the American taste, the American Chinese food was created in Chinatown, New York City.

Jade East was a Polynesian Chinese restaurant co-owned by my father and his partner in Towson, Maryland. The restaurant was a small replicate of the Trader Vic's, a high end restaurant inside the Statler Hilton, now known as the Capital Hilton. Jade East was a local, popular restaurant for romantic dates, celebratory events, and prom nights. When you walked through the door, you were magically transported to a tropical paradise with Don Ho's "Tiny Bubbles" playing in the back ground. The dimly lit room filled with the sweet aroma of tropical fruity rum drinks and the light scent of fresh orchids in the air. The dining room, with the ambiance of an island luau at dusk, was decorated with life size hand-carved Tiki statues from Hawaii, fishing net with colorful glass floating balls, and star fishes hanging over the ceiling. Bamboo rattan chairs with red leather seats placed neatly around tables and covered with freshly pressed tablecloth. Each Table had a huge rattan peacock chair typically reserved for the guest of honor. A row of hut-like booths aligned along one side of the dining room reserved upon request. The handsome waiters wore formal attire of black tie, pressed white shirt, and red dinner jacket. My father and his partner, in tailored matching pin striped suits, greeted the guests at the door and functioned as the maître d'. Jade East was known for its first class services, excellent Hawaiian Chinese cuisine with a French flare, and fancy tropical drinks such as Mai Tai, Scorpion, Blue Hawaii, Pina Colada, etc. The maître d' would personally flambé the Flaming Duck or the Rum Banana dessert at the table side with showman flare.

My first job experience at the age of thirteen was the hat check girl at Jade East. As the weather became cooler, the guests would check their coats at the front of the house. I greeted each customer with a charming smile, take their coats, and give them a number tag. If the male customer did not wear a proper suit, I would offer to lend him a dinner jacket to wear in the formal dining room. The tips were good for a thirteen year old.

At the age of fourteen, I was promoted to the hostess position with the responsibilities of assigning tasks to waiters who were all grown men. They had to listen to me because I was the owner's daughter. As Towson developed to be an university town, more casual restaurants started to pop up, including the Hooligan Pub next door to Jade East. The pretentious Jade East restaurant business started to slow down. Hence my father split with his partner, and became the sole owner of Jade East. As an effort to reduce over-head, my father put me through training at every station of the restaurant, from the front of the house to the kitchen operations. I learned to jump in anytime as hostess or busgirl or dish washer, if they were short of staff. Eventually I learned to help prep and cook a few simple dishes to cover the kitchen when the cook showed up late. At the age of fifteen, my step-brother and I were responsible for opening and closing the restaurant on weekends. So my parents could sleep in late or leave early on weekends, or when my father was too drunk to close the shop. I was learning restaurant management on the job, and took on responsibilities of an adult way before I was ready. My step-brother learned to be a bartender before the legal age. Whenever the business was slow, I was assigned to the back office to process credit cards and catchup on the book or run to the bank to get cash for the cashiers. I was also responsible for creating signage or marketing flyers for the restaurant using my art skills.

As teenagers my step-brother and I were often thrown into situations beyond our capabilities. One summer, my parents decided to take a vacation alone to Jamaica. They left my brother and I, the two oldest minors, in charge of the household of five kids and running the restaurant. The restaurant was burglarized the day after my parents left town. We suspected it was an inside job. Just imagine two nervous teenagers dealing with the police, trying to act as responsible mature adults. After I turned sixteen, with a legal work permit, I finally was able to work as a waitress, serve alcohol and make more tips. You see, we were never paid working for my parents in the family business. That was the American way, we were told by my parents. Looking back at the challenges in early life, ironically, I gained the skills that I leveraged in a successful professional career later in adult life. I am grateful for learning the valuable skills of running a small business, offering best-in-class customer services, managing difficult employees, and thinking on my toes under pressure.

But at the time, it was a miserable and embarrassing period for a teenager desperately wanting to be accepted by her peers. I missed out experiencing what it was like to be an American teenager. The worse part of working in Jade East was during prom nights, when I had to serve my fellow classmates! The girls always looked beautiful, dressed in fancy gowns with fresh wrist corsage; and the boys looked dapper in pastel color tuxedos and matching boutonniere. There I was in my waitress uniform and running between tables with a well-practiced smile of hospitality on my face. I cringed inside as they walked into the dining room. It was always awkward and humiliating. I secretly swore that I would never work in the restaurant business when I grow up. I wanted to be the customers.

Working in the restaurant was not my only job. My step-mother worked as a hairdresser in a beauty salon at the Scott's Corner, few miles down the York Road. I worked as the shampoo girl at the beauty shop on weekdays during every summer break. In addition to shampooing customers' hair, I provided the hairdresser assistance with perms and colors. I even served as a tester for the new electric perm machine. I had my straight long hair turned into the popular 1970's Afro look with a full head of tight curls. I also had a job as the cleaning lady for the beauty shop on weekends before I went to open the restaurant. Again, I worked for tips. I was motivated to save every penny to pay for my future college tuition and to get out of the house. As the family restaurant business slowed down and revenue declined, our parents demanded that my sister and I pay for our own rent. We were only high school age when we had to pay $200 per month each for our room and board. So, we worked, we worked, and we worked!

Self- Healing Moment

Shinrin-yoku: Forest Bathing

- Schedule time on your busy calendar to take a break out door.
- Go out door into the nature among the trees or neighborhood park, if you do not have a forest nearby.
- Take a leisurely walk to the forest, or among the trees.
- Look around you and breath as you walk mindfully.
- Notice your body soften with each breath.
- When you feel the urge, pulse and be still, gaze at a leaf or a bird, simply be one with the forest.
- Notice how you feel in your body after the forest bath.

14 DEEP SOUL PAIN

∞ ♥ ∞

"And into the forest I go, to lose my mind and find my soul."
-John Muir

High school was a dark period of my childhood. I became more self-aware of not meeting the standard as all the pretty American white girls around me. Asians are typically smaller in stature compared with American teenagers who looked like grown-ups in high school, especially girls with make-ups, breasts, and long legs. Although I had a round Onigiri face, I was short, flat chested with anorexic thinness. My dream of becoming an artist was crushed by the end of middle school. I was under tremendous pressure to take all the honors science classes, so I could be on the college track for pre-med as my parents dictated. Even my art teacher noticed and showed concerns about the shift in my artwork. I focused on creating realistic oil paintings as commissioned by clients instead of making arts that were imaginative and creative. I was still making decent income through commissioned art pieces. But, I stopped entering art contests completely. Outwardly, I was still the artsy "oriental" girl with the best personality award. I thought I was invincible handling increasing academic demands, shielding myself from domestic violence at home, and working all weekends to save money for college tuition and rent. After all, I came from the lineage of tigers, I am strong. I kept my eating disorder a secret from everyone.

The increasing stress at home and inadequate nutrition finally took its toll on my body. Overnight, I developed a hideous rash on my body, then my hair started to fall out in clumps. I was petrified that all the ugliness and secrets that I was hiding inside emerged to the surface for everyone to see! My parents finally took me to see a doctor and I was diagnosed with acute guttate psoriasis, a common presentation of psoriasis in children and adolescents. Once I started treatment, it took several months for my skin to return to normal. But I lost my long black hair. I hated to see my own image in the mirror, I felt extremely ugly, and I wanted to die.

All this self-loathing was happening in my head. Outwardly, I still smiled, got good grades, and did everything that I was supposed to do at home, at school, and at work. In the meantime, I became obsessed with researching on the topic of euthanasia, painless killing. I was seeking for a painless way to end my own life.

"Why are you into such a depressing topic?" My step-brother was the only person who noticed my obsession and made a comment as I checked out stacks of books on the topic from the library. Frankly, no one else noticed or cared.

I never told anyone and no one in my family knew until this book. As a teenager, I actually attempted suicide and failed. But everyone remembered the event simply as an accident. I signed up for driver's education during summer school. My parents had a fight the night before, my father was hungover, and my step-mother was too tired, so they refused to take me to the driver's education class in the morning as they agreed previously. The high school was much farther from our house than middle school. Most parents would gladly drive their kids to summer school, but not mine. So I found an old bike sitting in the garage and decided to get myself to class. I avoided York Road, because, everyone would see me, in such a small town. It would be another embarrassment if my classmates saw me.

I was getting more upset as I peddled the bike through the side roads. Finally, I reached a steep hill heading straight down toward a big tree at the bottom. I was exhausted by then, the hill seemed overwhelming in my life at that moment. I had a thought and a solution to all my problems, if I aim at the tree at the bottom of the hill, maybe the impact of riding high speed down-hill would end all this misery instantly. In my adolescent brain, perhaps without a fully developed prefrontal cortex, that was the perfectly right thing to do. So I pushed the bike to the very top of the hill, aimed for the tree and took off with full speed on the bike, flying down the hill. Fortunately, a pot hole half way down the steep hill, tipped my bike. I fell over and passed out on the grassy road side of the hill and avoid a potentially fatal crash.

I woke up in the ambulance, a man in uniform looking over me with a very concerned face. He kept saying "Keep your eyes open, stay awake, don't sleep. What is your name? We are taking you to the hospital." I later learned that a fireman drove by on the way to work, and saw my limp body bleeding at the side of the road. He called the ambulance immediately. It was a miracle that he drove by the remote road at the right time and saved me. After I was bandaged up in the hospital. I realized that I really did not want to die, but I was fleeing from the pain of living in a miserable and hopeless existence.

I fainted in the emergency room seeing the inner tissues down to the bone of my right forearm ripped open by the gravel. I had twenty one stiches and had to follow up by a plastic surgeon from Johns Hopkins. My step-mother finally came to the emergency room, she was in shock to see me in a bloody mess. The right side of my body hit the road, my face covered with abrasions, my arms and hands in bandages, the fingernails of my right hand were gone. My clothing covered with dry blood. It was a miracle that I did not crack my skull or break any bones. I truly believed that someone divine in the universe was watching me and protecting me.

The news of my accident traveled fast in high school. Everyone thought I had a car accident first day of driver's education class. I was showered with kindness and concerns from my classmates.

Resilience for me was the ability to rebound from adversity over and over. I was like a basketball, harder you pound on it, higher it would bounce up. Just like my earlier childhood serious illness. The failed suicide attempt woke me up again. I wanted to live.

I bounced back, kept going, and graduated with honors. My graduation present from my parents was a set of luggage. I guess that was also the American way. My childhood ended with a total ACEs score of seven. Unbeknownst to me at the time, the hidden resilience of the tiger spirit propelled me forward toward a destiny of seeing and discovering ways to reverse the harm.

Self-Healing Moment

A Letter to Your Younger Self after RAIN Meditation

- Find a quiet and comfortable place.
- Look around you and behind you.
- Find a sense of grounding.
- Connect with your breath.
- Close your eyes or simply soften your gaze.
- Scan your body with your breath.
- Notice any sensation in your body.
- **Recognize** it, name it. If it is hard to find a word, try to identify what it is, in shape or color.
- **Allow** it to be there. Give yourself the permission to feel and experience it in this safe space.
- **Investigate,** once you are okay to be with it…
  o Start to investigate it with kind intention… How does it feel in my body right now, any sensation?
  o Perhaps a little tightness at your heart center… place your hands where you feel something… your heart center perhaps… or tension in your shoulders.

- **Nurture** whatever you find, direct some loving kindness towards it. Give yourself a hug, or gentle massage.
- Continue for 2-3 minutes.
- Slowly let go of the RAIN.
- Go back to your breath, inhale deeply and exhale slowly and smoothly.
- Continue your normal breathing.
- Notice what happened in your tissues after the rain.
- **Write a letter to your-self when you were a child** – choose an age when you felt alone or sad. Be the compassionate nurturing adult for the child with the capacity and wisdom you embodies today.

15 PATH TO HEAL

∞ ♥ ∞

"Whenever you feel the world is closing on you, go to a quiet place that resides somewhere in your soul. Do not reason, analyze, or think, simply go."

-Unknown Author

"What would you like to be when you grow up? " Whenever someone asked me this question when I was a little girl about six or seven years old, I would answer, "I want to be a nun." I don't know where I got that idea. Perhaps it was because of the early Christian education. However, I recall my affinity for churches and temples ever since I can remember. I grew up with no one religion, my secular family practiced traditional ancestor worship at weddings and funerals. We also visited Catholic churches and befriended the local parish priests. Since my mother worked for the American Lutheran church in Taiwan, we celebrated Christmas at the Lutheran church. I loved visiting the local Catholic church nestled in the hills of Beitou. I remember my grandfather holding my little hand as we climbed the rustic stone steps to visit an old Catholic church on the top of the hill. We visited that church quite often because the priest was a family friend. As I entered the main chapel, the smell of the frankincense would transport me to a magical realm; the lights shining through the colorful stain glass windows dazzled me, and the gentle gaze of the Saint Mary statue evoked welcoming warm feelings in my little soul. As the grown-ups chatting in the courtyard, I often would sneak into the empty chapel and pretend I was praying as a nun. I also enjoyed a different calming sensation whenever I visited the traditional Buddhist temples. Chinese people living in Taiwan were predominantly Buddhist, and there were many majestic Buddhist temples around the island. The traditional Buddhist temples were also popular field trip destinations for schools. As a child, my memories were often connected with a scent. Sandalwood incense scent was the smell I associate with the Buddhist temples. The aroma of the sandalwood evoked a familiar peaceful feeling for my little soul. I especially enjoyed the monks or the nuns chanting at these temples. The deep humming vibration of the chants with the deep resonance of the gong brought soothing sensation to my entire being. I believe young children experiencing ACEs have the innate affinity to healing energy and self-soothing activities. In my case, these experiences led me to the dream of becoming a nun. Looking back at the black and white old photos, I came across a little girl with a serious gaze into the camera with namaste hands. A foreshadowing of an emerging yogini.

∞ ♥ ∞

As I grew older, I wanted to be an artist and designer. My middle school art teachers' praises, multiple art contest awards, and increasing commissions of my paintings as a teen artist, reinforced my desire to pursue the art field. I was merrily pursuing my dream, until it was shattered by my father and step-mother abruptly.

" You must be out of your mind! You want to be a starving artist?" My father shouted across the dinner table when the subject of what classes to take in high school came up serendipitously.

"You better think twice! We worked too hard to come to this country as immigrants, you must do better! All my friends' kids wanted to be doctors, lawyers, and respectful professions with good income." My father continued shouting at me with his eyes bulging with anger.

"I forbid you to even think about going to art school!"

Even though I was fully responsible for paying for my own college tuition without my parents' help, I backed down silently and squashed my dream of becoming an artist. I did not have the courage to stand up for myself or have the voice to speak my mind.

Unlike many little girls always dreaming to be a nurse, that thought never crossed my mind until the harsh reality hit that I needed to find a way to make a living and get out of this house as soon as possible. I knew I did not have the grades to get a full scholarship for medical school. I did my calculations and determined that if I go to a private college with higher tuition, I would have to live at home as a commuter. But if I go to a state university, my savings and working full time during the summer would afford both tuition plus room and board. It was a sure way out of the misery of living in a dysfunctional household with constant micro-aggressions and domestic violence. So I made the decision to go to Nursing School at the University of Maryland.

Life worked in mysterious ways. Baltimore Maryland was still a very segregated city, people of color lived in separate communities. I suspect the same practice applied to dorm assignments. So I was assigned an Asian American student as a roommate. The dorm monitor later told us that we were assigned the same dorm room, because our last names sounded Chinese. We were the only Asian students in that class. Interestingly, we were assigned the worst room in the freshmen dorm of the nursing school. Our dorm room wrapped around the elevator in an odd U-shape with loud pounding noises every time someone used the old elevator. But I was delighted to be out of my house and meeting someone who looked like me. My new roommate, Sharon, was an all American girl, born to Asian American parents whose ancestors immigrated to American in the 1800's during the building of the transcontinental railroad. Sharon was smart, pretty, and athletic. Most importantly, she was nice. Sharon became my best friend for life, and her parents kindly took me in as one more addition to their happy family of seven children. The Moy family gave me the first glimpse of a "normal" loving family.

I used to be so envious when Mr. and Mrs. Moy would stock up Sharon's dorm refrigerator with fresh fruits, home cooked meals, and snacks, when I could only afford Top Ramen, broccoli, and peanut butters. I jumped at every opportunity to go home with Sharon during school breaks. I loved sitting around the dinner table, after Mrs. Moy's delicious home cooking, listening to Mr. Moy's fascinating stories or practical life lessons. He probably told the same stories to his children over and over, they would quietly slip away, while I sat and listened to his pontification with utter delight. In the summer, I would get a full time job working in the University of Maryland Medical Center as a Nurse Assistant in the pediatric unit, so I could live in the dorm all summer and avoid going home.

Going to nursing school was the best life choice I made. In addition to the curriculum in medical, surgical, and public health nursing, I learned about how to access mental health resources. During the psych rotation, I tried to get my father to seek help for his alcohol addiction without success, but I was able to bring all my sisters to join the Al-Anon family support group to deal with my father's drinking problem and learn effective ways to cope.

Being on the downtown Baltimore campus gave me the space to practice self-care and enjoy campus life. The pub in the student union was a place where health science students from medical, dental, law, pharmacy and nursing schools took breaks from study. A break from study every Thursday night was my routine. Since I didn't touch alcohol, I hydrated with ice water and danced the night away. It was my own somatic therapy. Whenever I got the opportunity, I jogged to the harbor and breathed in the salty sea breeze. My eating disorder was under control, I binged and purged less. Going back home often triggered the old self destructive behaviors.

I got a job offer from Johns Hopkins Medical Center at its renowned Oncology Center, where the state of the art research for cancer treatment was conducted. The Human Resource Manager told me that my beautifully written resume stood out because I wrote it with my calligraphy pen. I worked on the unit specialized in phase one clinical trials for drugs used in bone marrow transplants (BMT). Phase one clinical trial studies were designed to find the highest dose of new treatment drugs that can be given safely and effectively without causing severe side effects. Most patients at the end stage of their cancer, would sign up to participate in phase one clinical trials studies voluntarily as their last hope. To be a part of the most innovative team to find treatment for cancer was an exciting opportunity for a newly graduated nurse.

University of Maryland Nursing education prepared me to be the best nurse, and Johns Hopkins Medical Center provided the stimulating academic environment for my professional growth. But no education prepared me emotionally to face death and dying. The 1980's was the golden era of nursing, where the primary nursing model was introduced. As a primary nurse, you were responsible for the patient's multidisciplinary care plan under the attending physician. The primary nurse was responsible for implementing the person-centered individualized plan of care around the clock, including medical care, nursing care, and psychosocial care needs. The primary nurse was the quarterback of the care team, and is responsible for implementing the care plan in coordination with the rest of the team from all three shifts. The nurse to patient ratio in that unit was one nurse to two patients. The primary nurse developed a very close trusting and caring relationship with the patients and their families, especially when these patients stayed in the BMT unit for months. They became your extended family.

Few months into the job, I lost my first patient, Cathy, who was only nineteen, few years younger than me.

I reported to my shift and discovered Cathy's bed empty. The parents were still in the room and told me she died during the night shift. They just took her body away. I did what the nursing school taught us not to do, I cried in front of the families. Not only did I cried uncontrollably in front of Cathy's parents, they had to hold me and comfort me. The charge nurse quietly pulled me out of the patient room and sat me down in the nursing station to calm myself down. I quickly had to collect myself, block off the pain, and return back to work taking care of patients newly assigned to me.

I was especially good with children; hence, they were frequently assigned to me. One of the side effects of high dose steroids in young children is psychosis. The sweetest child could turn into a little monster within hours, and the acting out behaviors continued until the treatment course ended. Frankie, a four year old boy, was my patient and suffered from steroid psychosis. I was the only nurse who could take care of him. He would yell, bite, and kick in a non-stop temper tantrum until he literally fell over with exhaustion. His mother always apologize profusely for her son's behaviors. This went on for months. After Frankie was discharged home, I saw him in the hospital cafeteria once. He came back for follow-up checkup and tests in the clinic. He saw me, eyes lit up, ran over and gave me the warmest hug with a big smile. The little monster turned into a delightful angel! That hug was the best reward of being a nurse seeing your patient getting well, especially a child back to being a kid again.

Since the clinical trial research unit was the last hope for many patients suffering from terminal cancer, I saw more people die in the unit than walking out like Frankie. Witnessing horrendous suffering of our patients, from the toxic side effect of chemotherapy trials and painful death, with no time to grieve, took a toll on the doctors and nurses including me. One patient, I name her Mary, was a young mother, just gave birth to a beautiful healthy baby. But she was diagnosed with end stage Chronic Myeloid Leukemia. She signed up for the clinical trial as a desperate reach for cure. Considering the risk of immunosuppression of the treatment, infants were not allowed to visit the unit, and the patients cannot venture out of their protective isolation. Mary saw her baby for the last time as she was admitted to the unit. Cytoxan, as name implied, a cytotoxic agent, was a brand new chemotherapy drug under clinical trial. One of its side effects was hemorrhagic cystitis, bleeding from the bladder. Since the early clinical trials were designed to establish highest effective dose, while titrating the dosage accordingly based on the side effects, Mary started with the highest dose possible. As her nurse, I literally observed helplessly, as a beautiful young mother, withered away in excruciating pain physically and emotionally. Mary died a horrific death, the lining of her internal organs, including her bladder, literally sluffing off every time she used the bed side commode or vomited. She bled to death, and was utterly alone at the last moment of her life.

I was suffering from compassion fatigue and

vicarious trauma. I started to question if nursing was the right profession for me given my limited capacity to deal with the stress. As nurses we were taught Kubler-Ross stages of grief, and learned how to support our patients and their family with the loss of a loved one. But we never learned how to process grief for the death of our patients whom we cared for months and some over a year. We never gave ourselves enough time to be vulnerable and practice self-care. I remember feeling extreme sadness, and often cried all the way on the drive home after a long busy shift. Sometimes, the nurses would hit the pubs after a difficult night to console each other over drinks and chain smoking. I burned out after one year as a Registered Nurse in the BMT unit. The pain of seeing your patients suffer and die one by one, even for the benefit of discovering a cure for cancer for the greater good, was too much to bear. I fled again.

I understood exactly how the health care professionals and frontline workers had to endure during the peak of COVID19 pandemic. Despite the years of professional training and dedication to heal others, we are also vulnerable human beings with our own trauma. I became one of the strongest advocates at the workplace for offering toxic stress buffering resources and teaching self-care to the health care providers and patient- facing health care workforce, especially those young ones just entering the noble profession of Do No Harm.

Self-Healing Moment

Self-Compassion Journal and Mindfulness Practice

- Dedicate a journal as your self-compassion journal.
- At the end of the day, take a moment for yourself in a quiet place.
- Review today's events in your mind.
- Write down anything that you are grateful about.
- Write down one kind gesture that someone expressed toward you or vice versa.
- Write down anything that you felt bad about or what made you sad.
- Pulse, close your eyes if you choose.
- Take a deep breath in, and a slow smooth breath out.
- Use your breath to scan your body, notice any sensation.
- Notice, name it if you can, with acceptance and without any self judgement.
- Direct your breath to the part of your body that felt tight or constricted.
- Place your hand on the part of the body with the sensation or give yourself a hug.
- Invite some softness to that part of your body with your breath.

- Continue few more breath cycles.
- Return to your journal.
- Write down what emerges from your heart.
- Express kindness, love, and acceptance of yourself as a human being.
- Tell yourself and affirm: I did my best work today. Tomorrow is a new day.

16 YOU DO NOT BELONG

∞ ♥ ∞

"You do not need to seek freedom in some distant land, for it exists within your own body, heart, and mind, and soul."

-B.S.K. Iyengar

In the 1970's and 1980's, life was lonely for Chinese American young adults living in the US, especially if you lived far away from large Chinese communities such as Chinatown of New York City, San Francisco, or Los Angeles. Most Chinese American communities were small and lacking any Asian American identity. Hence growing up as an "minority" in Baltimore, I always felt like an outsider even though people were polite and nice to you outwardly. The common greeting was always, "Where are you from?" meaning you do not belong here. While in Nursing school, I had many opportunities of dating white medical students, dental students, and law students. I suspect some boys just wanted to satisfy their curiosity of dating a Chinese girl, and those relationships always ended quickly after one date. Whenever the relationship progressed to a more serious level, perhaps time to meet the families, the relationship often came to a halt. Most traditional American families in Baltimore, Maryland at that time were not open to mixed race relationships. Frankly, I was also secretly ashamed of my dysfunctional family to bring anyone home to meet my parents.

Many Chinese American parents send their American born young adults to Overseas Chinese Language Training and Study Tour. A government sponsored program in Taiwan to acquaint or re-acquaint young people of Chinese descent, living in other parts of the world, with Chinese culture and language. So when Sharon, my best friend from Nursing School, suggested that we go on the tour together, after hearing rave reviews from her brother, I jumped at the idea as I desperately needed a break from dealing with death and dying in the hospital. The thought of visiting the island of my birth was enticing and nostalgic. By that time my entire extended Chang families had all immigrated to the US.

The six weeks Study Tour, organized by China Youth Corps, included room and board, cultural activities, language and art classes, plus escorted trips to various tourist destination of Taiwan. The host treated the overseas Chinese young adults as diplomats with VIP treatments. The Study Tour was a political strategy of the Taiwan Oversees Community Affairs Council to proactively develop favorable relations with overseas compatriots. The "Love Boat" was the nick name for the Study Tour. I did encounter a few crushes, but truth be told, most of the Chinese Americans on the tour were in the final year of attending universities or new graduates, they were much too young. I already had one year of employment under my belt. I felt like a tired old soul jaded with work-life experiences. Sharon on the other hand, met her future husband, a handsome Chinese American from California, on the "Love Boat."

Although Taiwan was my birth place, growing up under the care of grandparents, my young life was sheltered and limited to my hometown and the capital of Taipei. I never ventured to the rest of the island including the beaches. Returning a decade later, I finally saw the beautiful island with fresh eyes and experienced the friendly locals' hospitality. I vaguely felt a sense of belonging, even though I no longer had any immediate family members living on the island.

At the end of the Study Tour, I was very reluctant to return to the sad existence and dysfunctional family in Baltimore. Although part of my ACE score started on this island, those who harmed me were all in the US now. I was still fleeing and searching for my path. I told Sharon to get on the airplane returning back to the US without me.

Luckily, I had one of my grandfather's formal university connections on the island, who owned a pottery and ceramic art center in the Yingge Village of the Shulin Township located in the southwest of Taipei. As an apprentice in the ceramic art center, l worked side-by-side with the local potters and craftsmen. I learned how to use pottery wheels and mold a lump of clay into a symmetrical and functional vessel. I could spend hours on the pottery wheel, peddling with my feet, feeling the smooth cool clay between my fingers, and noticing how a slight shift of my palms can change the shape entirely or even destroy the perfect pottery. The mindful focus of a potter was soothing to my entire being, and I craved for the sense of anchoring to a deeper root. It always amazed me to see how the seemingly dull coats of glazes would turn into brilliant shades of colorful jewels after the intense heat in the kiln. The art center frequently invited famous local artists and calligraphers to offer classes to the potters and workers. These enrichment classes not only served as welcomed social events at the company, but also promoted creative exchanges to help perfect the craftsmen's brush painting skills and stimulated more ideas for new original pottery pieces.

I loved participating in those classes. I kept several original paintings by the local artists created especially for me with their name signed in beautiful brushstrokes. When I was not working on the pottery wheel, I enjoyed working alongside with the workers of the porcelain dolls. These classical Chinese porcelain dolls were created by molds. After the dolls came out of the molds while the clay was still damp, the workers would use smooth bamboo chisels to smooth out the surface and seams. These miniature dolls were only two and a half inches, and fitted perfectly in my palm. I imagined they were fairies in disguises as I meticulously finishing the clay surface of these little dolls. After the porcelain dolls were covered with a coat of white glaze, we painted their hair and faces and adorned their bodies with very fine brushes. The workers would comment about the big round eyes I painted on the doll faces instead of the traditional almond shaped eyes. Unconsciously, every dolls I painted with loving care looked like me when I was a baby girl.

Many workers lived in a village nearby. We became friends. One elderly gentleman, in charge of calligraphy, invited me to his village one day. I sat on the back of his old bicycle, clutching the metal frame with my dear life, as he meandered skillfully through the busy city street into a traditional village. I have never been to a local village, I felt like traveling back in time surrounded by the old 三合院 Sānhéyuàn, a traditional Taiwanese court yard home, typically a U-shaped house with three sides, surrounding a courtyard. My friend took me to his old home and showed me all the calligraphy and Chinese paintings by his father and grandfather. He clearly was very proud of his literary lineage. I was very touched that he took the time to show me his treasures. Since my grandfather was a calligrapher as well, I appreciated the beauty of each character and felt the energy of the ancestors through the brush strokes.

In addition to the apprenticeship, I earned pocket money by giving English guided-tours in the pottery museum, and teaching conversation English to high-school students. I got a room at the big house belonging to my aunt's in-laws in Taipei. Secretly, I still had the fantasy of pursuing my dream and living a simple life as a care free artist.

∞ ♥ ∞

One of the Study Tour counselors stayed in touch while I was in Taiwan. We became friends. He would stop by frequently to see me after work, and we would chat for long hours at the tea shops. He was very curious about my seemingly very care free American spirit. Not many Chinese young adults would quit a respectful job, travel far away from home, and spend time aimlessly to indulge self-interests. Our friendship quickly morphed into a romantic interest. He was my first real Chinese boy-friend. He kind of resembled the famous Kung Fu actor, Bruce Lee, with dark frame glasses that gave him a serious mature demeanor on a boyish face, I found him attractive in a very un-American way.

He introduced me to the afternoon tea dance, where young people would flock to the dance hall in the afternoon after school, just to dance. We tried street vendor food that I was never allowed growing up as a child. My grandparents had forbidden us eating anything from the street vendors, because they felt the food was not hygienically prepared, and we would get sick. One of the popular street foods in Taiwan was beef noodle soup similar to the Vietnamese Pho. Slurping savory beef noodle soup, sitting on the wooden bench of the street vendor, surrounded by bustling night street sounds, was an all-new experience to me. On a humid hot summer day, sharing a huge bowl of shaved ice, piled up high with toppings of preserved fruits, sweet red beans, lotus seeds, dripping with thick sweet milk, was the most refreshing heavenly treat. Oh, the fresh papaya smoothies, another tropical favorite…I was simply soaking up the experience with all my senses moment by moment. My dark secrets were all so far away.

Since we were becoming more serious in our relationship, we even discussed the possibility of him joining me in the US. He wanted me to meet his parents and siblings over a home cooked dinner by his mother. We traveled by train to a village in Hualien, south of the busy Taipei. My counselor came from a very patriotic family. Both parents were active in the local community. They worked hard to support all their children through university. They were very proud of their only one son, being selected by the Overseas Community Affairs Council to serve as a counselor Study Tour, a great honor. The visit was polite and cordial with some questions about my families in the US. I respectfully answered their questions with some vagueness and reservation. I understood that traditional Chinese families did not think highly of families of divorces.

∞♥∞

A few days later, I received a letter from my boyfriend's mother. Basically, she asked me, in a very polite way, to stop seeing her son. She felt that it was wrong that I filled his head with ideas of going to the US. She pointed out that my American education and practices were not compatible with their traditional Chinese family.

"If you are a true Chinese women who loved her country and heritage, you would not think twice about staying and serving your own country." My boyfriend's mother ended the letter, basically stating, "You do not belong here". That was the end.

My fantasy life was over, my heart was shattered, not so much by the abrupt ending to a sweet short romance, but the stark reminder that I belonged nowhere. I was not good enough to be a Chinese, and I was not good enough to be an American. I did not belong here or there.

I called my mother, Elsie, in Hawaii. Because my funds were depleted and I needed a ticket to fly home. She flew to Taiwan as soon as she booked the first flight, and took me back to the US. She did not ask what happened, and I did not elaborate. Secretly, she was glad that I came back to my senses, ended my bohemian life style, and came back to America, the beautiful country.

Passing through California, on the way to Baltimore, I decided that I needed to move west and have a fresh start. I worked three months as a per diem nurse on a medical-surgical unit in a local community hospital, saved enough money, bought a red Volkswagen Rabbit, learned to drive stick-shift, and headed to Los Angeles, California.

Self-Healing Moment

Three Self Caring Breaths Practice

- Find a quiet place.
- Place both hands on your heart center.
- Take a deep breath in, feel the chest expanding, your heart opening.
- Slowly breath out...dedicate this <u>first caring breath</u> to yourself as a child, and
- Be grateful that you have this moment to care for the inner child.
- Bring to mind, your present self.
- You might need to settle in the present moment first. Feel the ground beneath you, look around you and behind you.
- Dedicate your <u>second caring breath</u> to your present self.
- Take a deep breath in, and a slow breath out with care and kindness towards that person.
- Bring to mind, your future self.
- Take a deep breath in, feeling the <u>third caring breath</u> filling up your lungs, notice the sensations.
- Breath out slowly and feel the sensation at your heart center, what does it feel like to feel free and cared for as your future self?

- Imagine the past, present, and future selves merging into one, the embodiment of wisdom and loving kindness.
- Go back to you normal breathing.
- Savor this moment as long as you desire.

17 THE BUTTERFLY EFFECT

∞ ♥ ∞

"Gratitude unlocks the fullness of life. It turns what we have into enough and more.

It turns denials into acceptance, chaos into order, confusion to clarity."

-Melody Beattie

Life works in mysterious ways. My mental health seemed to improve as soon as the California sun kissed my face. I felt an instant lightness as I breathed in the pleasant warm dry air. I was so delighted to be offered a job at the renown Children's Hospital of Los Angeles (CHLA) on the Hematology Oncology Unit, where the children received proven cancer treatments, or participated in clinical studies designed specifically for children.

"How can you take care of children with cancer? It is so depressing!" People often commented when they find out I took care of children with cancer.

On the contrary, I found children's innate affinity for joy and their ability to play in the moment, despite their suffering, inspirational. Many children diagnosed with catastrophic conditions or managing inherited medical conditions since birth became wise souls beyond their biological age. I'd much rather take care of children with cancer than adults with cancer. Also I found that pediatricians, in general, are more person-centered and family oriented than any other specialties in medicine. They are not afraid to be vulnerable, be human, and have fun on the job. I spent sixteen years at CHLA after relocating to California.

Since my mother's Chang family including her father, the Paper Tiger, and his offspring were all settled in California, all of sudden I had extended families. I found a one-bed room apartment in a culturally diverse San Gabriel Valley and started a new life. I then started getting to know the other cousins of the Chang family that I lost contact with after my mother left me as a young child.

As I turned twenty five years old and still single, my anxious relatives started to be concerned that I will be an old maid. One of my aunts took upon herself to be the matchmaker. Her best friend, Mrs. Ha, a Vietnamese Chinese lady, had three unmarried and eligible sons. They organized a family dinner at my aunt's house with the intention of introducing me to Co, the oldest son. When we first met, I was impressed with his good looks and smooth California sun tanned complexion. He was fluent in French, English, Cantonese and Mandarin Chinese. As we were introduced, I sensed an air of arrogance. Clearly, he was equally annoyed as me for this old fashioned arrangement of his mother and my aunt. Ironically, I had a very positive impression of Mrs. Ha. She held my hands warmly right away, and adored me as a new daughter she always wanted. She was kind, warm, and unpretentious. It was refreshing to meet someone like her very unlike the matriarch figures in the Chang family.

With both family's encouragement, Co and I started to date reluctantly. We were completely opposite in our personality, I was talkative, he was very quiet. I liked to discuss conceptual ideas, he liked to discuss factual information in great details; I enjoyed classical arts, he enjoyed abstract arts. But we both loved good food, art museums, music, and open nature. Co was very sporty, he swam like a fish and loved downhill skiing. I admired his adventurous spirit deep in the sea and high up the ski slopes. Whereas I literally get anxiety attacks when my feet cannot touch the ground, in the sea or on a ski lift. He had to rescue me many occasions.

I re-called a scary but comical incident that might have changed the trajectory of our relationship. Co wanted to teach me how to ski and took me to Mammoth on a perfect winter day. I was a very awkward and amateur skier. Co seemed to be overly confident and decided to take me on a black diamond run. The trouble started on the ski lift. I got on the lift, but my ski accidentally knocked Co off the ski lift, as the ski lift was heading up to the black diamond slope. I started to panic as the ski lift continued up the slope, I had no idea when to get off the lift or what I would do up there? So I jumped off the ski lift that was at least two stories from the ground. Luckily, I landed on soft powdery snow. The ski lift operator stopped the ski lift to make sure I was not hurt. I felt my face burning red from embarrassment as all the seasoned skiers staring down at me from the lift. I did not want to give up so soon, so Co and I successfully took the next ski lift up to the top of the black diamond slope. Since I was a rookie at skiing, I kept going cautiously crisscrossing the ski slope vertically, as Co skied down the challenging black diamond slope effortlessly. He came back up the slope and skied back down a few rounds, while I was still crisscrossing the black diamond slope slowly. I might have looked very focused and calm, but I was hiding my fear of falling. Finally, the sun started setting, the sky was turning gray, the temperature was dropping, I was still crisscrossing half way up the slope. Finally, Co had to get the ski patrol to fetch me with the snowmobile and get me off the ski slope before the nightfall.

We did not fall in love at the first sight. But I suspect surviving the ordeal of the ski trip might have brought us closer. It took months of old fashion courting before we both let go of our resentments of this "arranged match." When we finally kissed for the first time, we both felt a strong chemistry attraction and unexplainable connection. However, the deciding factor of marrying Co, was actually Mrs. Ha, his mother. She treated me nicer than my own mother treated me, she was the complete opposite of the image I had of the traditional Chinese mother-in-law based on Ching-Ma's story and how she treated her two daughters-in-law. Whenever I visited Mrs. Ha, she always prepared a delicious spread of Cantonese cuisines banquet style. She was delighted that I took conversation Cantonese lessons at the Chinatown, so I can converse with Mrs. Ha in her language and understand her stories.

Co and I got married after dating for only six months. We got married at the beautiful Wayfarers Chapel, better known as the "Glass Church" designed by Frank Lloyd Wright. A unique glass chapel seamlessly blended in its beautiful natural surroundings perched on the cliff of Rancho Palos Verdes overlooking the Pacific Ocean. It was the perfect venue for us, for we both appreciate modern architecture and unique designs. The formal Christian wedding ceremony included one hundred close families and friends. When I removed the white wedding dress, I changed into a traditional long qipao made with embroidered roses on bright pink silk fabric. The delicate fabric was picked by my mother-in-law' and handmade by her seamstress from Chinatown. After adorning more pure gold necklaces and bracelets given to me by Co's other aunties, I was ready for the real celebration of a big traditional Chinese wedding banquet. We invited over three hundred guests, including our co-workers of doctors, nurses, and engineers, to share the delicious ten course feast and joy of our union. The wedding celebration was followed by a sweet honeymoon at Carmel. Co and I completed another rites of passage expected by our traditional Chinese families. We were both young and clueless to what awaited us as married couples.

I did not have the scientific knowledge about ACEs and trauma at the time, hence I could not have known the impact of our generational trauma, my ACEs, and his Vietnam war trauma would intersect in our relationship after marriage. If I had the same knowledge and wisdom as I have today, I would have insisted that we both start professional therapy and healing process before getting married. We would go into the marriage fully resourced with trauma-informed self-regulation tools to face the life journey together with mutual care and compassion. We would have a deeper understanding of what happened to us and how that influenced our actions and choices. Perhaps the greater purpose of me not knowing what I know now, is the opportunity to share my story through our own trials and tribulations as survivors, partners, and parents.

I am grateful that it is not too late to share our journey with a trauma-informed lens. For the next generation of singles who are searching for the life partner, I hope you will tap into the resources available to you, so we all have a greater awareness to heal our trauma together. Remember, at the end of the day, love always prevails.

Self-Healing Moment

Butterfly Breath

This self-care practice is inspired by the Butterfly Effect. A term attributed to the work of Edward Norton Lorenz (1917-2008) a mathematician and meteorologist. A small initial change, such as a distant butterfly flapping its wings, could lead to a significantly different outcome in the world. May your butterfly breaths lead to lasting healing of your mind, body, and soul.

Grounding

- Find a comfortable seat.
- Place both feet on the ground, feel free to take off your shoes and socks, so you can feel the earth beneath your feet.
- Place both hands palms down on your lap.
- Lower your you gaze or close your eyes if you like.

Check in

- Take a moment to Check In - notice how you are feeling right now.
- Find a word to name it.
- When we can recognize it and call it what it is, we defuse its power and hold on us.

Body Awareness

- Bring your awareness to your feet, find a sense of grounding.
- Feel the chair underneath your thighs supporting you.
- Lengthen your torso from the base of your spine towards the crown of your head.
- Row your shoulders up, back and down - release your shoulder blades down your back.
- Soften your face and unclench your jaw.
- Cross your arms at your heart center.
- Give your shoulders and upper arms gentle squeezes with your hands.
- Continue as long as you need to feel some release of the tensions from your shoulders.
- Keep arms crosses at the heart center and rest palms on the upper arms.
- Find stillness.

Breath Awareness

- Bring your awareness to your breath without changing it, simply observe.
- Notice the quality and texture of your breathe.
- Inhale - notice the cool air entering your nostril, rib cage and belly expanding.
- Exhale - notice belly and rib cage drawing in, and a slightly warmer air exiting the nostril.

- Continue with your own breath cycles effortlessly.
- Be in touch with the full duration of each breath going out, and notice the slight pulse at the top and bottom of each breath.
- Add the movement of the palms as butterfly wings.
- Inhale - gently lift the palms up away from the upper arms.
- Exhale - gently lower the palms back on the upper arms.
- You are not so much thinking about the breath or the breath sensations, rather you are feeling the sensations as butterfly wings fluttering in synchronization with your breaths.
- Let go of the desire to control your effort, just float with the butterfly wings and your breaths.
- Breathe in and breathe out.
- Give yourself over completely to the breath sensations, moment by moment by moment.
- Continue the butterfly breaths as long as you wish or until you feel your body softens with a calm sensation.

18 UNCONDITIONAL LOVE

∞ ♥ ∞

"There is a hidden seed of greater wholeness in everyone and in everything.

We serve life best when we water it and befriend it. When we listen before we act."

-Rachel Naomi Remen

I am forever grateful to be blessed with people in my life that countered the harm of my ACEs and filled the gaps of unconditional love. My mother-in-law was one of them. Chi was the seventh child and the only daughter of the Ly family. She was born in the province of Canton. Her parents died when she was a very young child. She always told us the sadness of not having a mother to love and protect her. Hence, she always adored children and loved all her children and grandchildren unconditionally. Most of her brothers immigrated to Vietnam seeking better economic opportunities. Chi was left behind and lived with her oldest brother and sister-in-law, where she helped out with cooking and house work. She started learning all the traditional Cantonese cooking and use of herbs at a young age.

When the Second Sino Japanese war erupted in China, Chi was only eleven years old. Although the atrocities and the war was happening in Shanghai and Manchuria, Northeast of Canton, the horror stories of the war and the increasing uncertainty prompted her brother to send her to Vietnam. Chi arrived to Can Tho Vietnam at the age of sixteen and lived with her other brothers' family. Can Tho was a city in southern Vietnam, located on the left bank of the Hau Giang river, a place of busy commerce and opportunities.

Contrary to the traditional medicine practices, Chi believed in western medicine and treatments. Hence, she went to nursing school and became a nurse at the Chinese speaking hospital in the Cho Lon, Vietnam's Chinatown. She worked in the obstetric unit and helped deliver babies for the Vietnamese Chinese families of Cantonese descent. Chi met her future husband Luan Ha, the second and younger son of a third generation Vietnamese Chinese family, who lived down the street in Can Tho. Later they married in Saigon and moved to Cho Lon.

The Ha family had a thriving business of manufactured and distributed household products, headed by the oldest son, my husband Co's uncle. As typical Chinese family, every one contributed to the family business, his aunt helped with book keeping, while my father-in-law, Luan was responsible for collecting payments from the merchants. The close knit families of the two brothers and wives, lived nearby and raised their children together as one big family. After marriage and having three sons, Chi was responsible for cooking for the large family as well as the factory workers, while she continued to work as a visiting nurse part time. As the third generation of Vietnamese Chinese, the Ha family continued the Chinese traditions, passing on Taoism and Confucius philosophy, while making sure all their children were educated in classical Chinese language in addition to French and Vietnamese.

The Ha children of both brothers, typically attended French or Vietnamese schools in the morning, and attended Chinese school in the afternoon. However, from the Vietnamese government perspective, the ethnic Chinese people in Cho Lon, were a close group and not willing to assimilate to the Vietnamese culture. Also the successful Chinese economy was viewed as a threat by the locals. Hence, the ethnic Chinese children were often bullied by the local Vietnamese children in school.

After the French colonial rule in Indochina ended

in 1954, Vietnam was divided into two parts. The North Vietnam was under the full control of Vietnamese Communist Party led by Ho Chi Minh, with its capital located in Hanoi; and the South Vietnam remained under the control of the former Vietnamese emperor, Boa Dai, with its capital located in Saigon. After the French departed, the US army moved into Saigon with the intention to stop the spread of Communism in Vietnam, and started the Vietnam War. Ironically in Vietnam, the history book recorded it as the American War.

The Ha family business based in Saigon, known as Ho Chi Minh City today, continued to thrived surrounded by US troop protection. But the war was happening in the country side and underground surrounding Saigon. For those who lived in Saigon, they were shielded from witnessing the guerrilla warfare. But en route to the country side, they could not ignore the tension all around. The younger Ha brothers recalled accompanying their father to collect payments from the village merchants and driving through the country side. Their car would be stopped by road blocks, they would routinely jump off the car, and hide at the side of the road until the bombing and helicopters passed. The sound and smell of the war was in the air with invisible enemies. Although the children were oblivious, the parents were worried for the Ha boys as they were reaching the age to be drafted into the army and be at the frontline of the war.

One by one, their uncle arranged for all the sons to

study abroad, to Taiwan, France, and the US to avoid the draft, while all the girl cousins were left behind. The arrangement required a lot of gold bars, for the Vietnamese government officials were all taking bribes.

My husband Co, for some odd reason, decided to study in the US instead of the original plan to study in France, as he was fluent in French, not English. A life decision that enabled our paths to cross. He had to re-take all his exam in English and barely passed. He left Vietnam December 1974 on a student VISA, headed to a private university in North Carolina. He celebrated the Lunar New Year in Taiwan with his younger brother and arrived in the US February 1975. Two months later, Communist took over Vietnam on April 30, 1975. Co did not have to experience the hardship endured by the rest of his family, which was leaving Vietnam as refugees, the Boat People. But the experience of arriving to a foreign land, that you no longer have a country, and not knowing when or if you will ever see your family again, was an extremely traumatic experience for a nineteen year old. I believe Co suffered from symptoms of Post-Traumatic Stress Disorder (PTSD) that was never diagnosed or treated. Since the fall of Vietnam to this date, Co still suffers nightmares and cold sweats from the memories that still haunt him. Some nights, waken by his silenced scream and whimper of the war nightmares, all I could do was hold him close until dawn.

∞ ♥ ∞

As ethnic Chinese in Vietnam who owned businesses, they were the target of the new communist regime. Co's uncle immediately started to organize an escape plan by boat after the fall of Vietnam. He purchased a large fishing boat with his gold. Unfortunately, someone tipped off the Communists and the plan was aborted. But instead of Co's uncle, my father-in- law was arrested. He confessed that he was the organizer of the boat escape, so his older brother's life could be spared and he could continue the covert escape plan.

In 1975, the escapes were all poorly organized during the mass exodus. Once the Communists realized the people from the South were leaving the country illegally by boats, they decided to clamp down the departure and profit. In exchange for the official permit to leave, the refugees had to sign-over their property, give up gold, and valuable belongings. The new law caused the Ha family to re-think their escape strategy. Instead of all leaving on one boat, they decided to leave in phases and include family members as well as friends. Since Chi's husband was in prison, she decided to be the last to leave, while holding on to their home. In case the escape failed, the Ha family still had a place to return. She told us the stories of keeping lights on and making noises as if the house was still occupied by the large family. Every day she lived under the fear of being discovered and arrested.

Co's uncle, organized several boat trips and helped

all his families, extended families, and friends escape the Communist Vietnam by Boat. Chi finally escaped by boat to Malaysia in 1978. A few years later Co's father was released from the prison. My father-in-law was the last person to leave Vietnam on a boat. He never said much about his experience in the prison, but the scar of the ordeal was deeply hidden. Although he never drank alcohol or used any substance to numb his painful memories, I recall witnessing a disproportionate explosion of violence and anger that seemed to be triggered by his traumatic memory. One time, my young daughter and I were petrified, as he chased my husband, his own son, with a butcher knife across the living room of our home. We never really knew what triggered his outbursts of violence. Luckily, my mother-in-law was able to calm him down.

Although my story does not elaborate on the hardships, the pirate attacks, rape of young girls, and loss of lives experienced by the Boat People, all the trauma they suffered and the resilience collectively were all part of the AAPI legacy in the Chang Ha family. The trauma as refugees escaping by boats still lived in the bodies of those who survived and in the communities they shared.

Chi, our Mah-Mah, has passed when I write this chapter as a tribute to her unconditional love. She lived a life of faith, humility and gratitude. Her loving kindness touched so many lives beyond our family. Mah-Mah cared for family with no expectation. She loved everyone. She prayed for all her grandchildren every day. She treated her friends with the same love and respect. She was a very special human being. But, her body kept the score. She suffered from multiple chronic illnesses, finally her kidney and heart failed.

She left her children and grandchildren with strong foundational values. According to Mah-Mah, human beings are a small part of this universe, we must learn to care and love layer by layer, starting with the individual, family, community, society, country, globe, and finally the universe. Love starts with family and starts with good food. Feeding people generously was Mah-Mah's way to connect with people and show her love.

Self-Healing Moment

Meditation of Breathing Love

- Find a quiet place and a comfortable seat.
- Find a sense of grounding.
- Take three cleansing breaths, inhale through the nose, and exhale through the mouth.
- Return to normal breathing in and out through your nose.
- Inhale peace, exhale love.
- Inhale acceptance, exhale love.
- Inhale joy, exhale love.
- Inhale acceptance, exhale love.
- Inhale compassion, exhale.
- Inhale truth, exhale love.
- Inhale curiosity, exhale love.
- Inhale connection, exhale love.
- Inhale kindness, exhale love.
- Inhale forgiveness, exhale love.
- Inhale gratitude, exhale love.
- Inhale unity, exhale love.
- Inhale love, exhale love.
- Sit and notice.
- Give yourself a big loving hug.

19 MOTHERHOOD

∞ ♥ ∞

"A gender equal world means identifying as a woman does not make her vulnerable or constrained, and the intersections of her gender with all her other attribute make her more interesting, successful, and strong."

-Rena Greifinger

I grew up with a set of implicit values for a modern woman - how pretty you look, how well you cook, how many sons you give birth to, and how successful you are professionally. The expectations of entering motherhood right after marriage was another rite of passage in the traditional Chinese culture. Despite the fact that we were all raised to be modern American women, the unspoken expectation was weaved into the fabric of our core values. Under the pretense that the generation grew up in America and should do better than the last generation, our immigrant parents added the expectation of a successful professional career to the list of the traditional values.

Since the strategic marriage to the Ha family, I was relieved of the pressure to have a male heir. However, I still had a self-imposed time line of having my first child before the age of thirty, in addition to finishing graduate school, and advancing in my career. Other than the text book knowledge of infants development and maternal child health from nursing school, I had no role model or any clue about how to be a mother and raise a child.

Ironically, the work-work-work ethic instilled in me by my immigrant parents gave me the false confidence that I could do it all. So I followed my time line to get pregnant with no further consideration that I just started my first management position as the Assistant Nurse Manager of the brand new Bone Marrow Transplant (BMT) unit at CHLA; I was going through graduate school full time; and we purchased a fixer-upper as our first house with our own savings. Having a professional job, achieving higher education, and owning a house, all three boxes checked. We were living the American dream - Everything is possible in this country as long as you work hard!

Since I was accustomed to be the first "other", I was enjoying the novelty of being the only pregnant student at the graduate school. I had the false perception that everything was under my control. My life was on track and on schedule. But, my baby decided to arrive several weeks early on the day of the mid-term exam! Despite all the birthing preparation and Lamaze classes, nothing prepared me for twenty four hours of labor. Finally, my doctor suggested C-section, but he allowed me to try one more push. To everyone's surprise, my first baby girl, Stephanie, came through the birth canal and saved me from the C-section. The nurse took the new born away immediately to make sure she was thriving after the long birthing process. Co had the honor of cutting her umbilical cord as the new dad. He could not hold back tears of joy as he handed our baby Stephanie to me. Seeing this tiny living being, who was part of me for months, opened her eyes and now gazed into mine. The first mother-baby gaze must be a biological design to unleash the floodgate of love that I never knew I had in my heart. I felt the fierce instinct of the tigress ready to protect this precious being with my life.

Nothing prepared me for the emotional roller coaster ride of the next few days in the hospital. Stephanie developed severe jaundice, a condition attributed to babies born before thirty-eight weeks' gestation. A newborn's immature liver can't remove bilirubin quickly enough, and supposedly the jaundice can be caused by the mother's breast milk. The thought that my breast milk was making my baby ill was a distressing thought. Since Stephanie was slightly pre-term and with jaundice, the doctor decided to discharge me home first, while keeping my baby in the hospital. The protective instinct of a new mother rose up in me, I stood my ground and refused to be discharged home without my baby. The postpartum depression kicked in, I was an emotional wreck. I was probably the worst patient on the Obstetric unit. The doctor finally let me stay in the hospital and the nurses left me alone. Every time I saw my baby with her jaundice yellow complexion, I felt overwhelming guilt and helplessness, and I cried and cried the entire hospital stay. Luckily, it was before managed care and we had two indemnity health plan coverages. Hospital length of stay was not an issue.

Finally, a week later, the doctor agreed to send Stephanie home with around the clock bilirubin light, and I had to keep her hydrated to decrease the bilirubin level in her blood. I had a home health nurse visiting me daily to prick her little heel and check the bilirubin level to determine when I can resume breast feeding. The fact that my breast milk caused harm to my own baby, deflated the little confidence I had as a new mother. All the books I studied did not prepare me for the lack of confidence as a mother. So, I did what I knew how, be a nurse. I was on all three shifts. I still have the chart that I kept of Stephanie's daily intake and output every hour, her signs and symptoms, lab results, and notes for weeks.

The responsibility of being a new parent weighed

heavily on us as young parents. Co was still trying to get our new home ready for the baby when we brought Stephanie home. We both did not know how to express our anxiety or how to support each other. He was stoic and silent. Although my mother visited us, other than rocking her granddaughter so I could catch a nap, she was not much help. She always had a nanny who took care of her newborn babies and bottle feeding was the modern trend during her era.

My mother-in-law seemed to be the only person who knew what to do. On my first day home, she made bone broth infused with all the Chinese herbs beneficial for postpartum recovery. She also made special dishes to help stimulate breast milk production, in addition to deliciously nutritious herb soups. I remember the honey ginger chicken and wine braised chicken with red rice as two of my favorite dishes. She adored Stephanie, her first granddaughter. I was deeply grateful for having such a loving mother-in-law and grandmother for my girl. She was my only role model of a nurturing mother. But at the same time, I felt more inadequate as a mother, whenever I was around her.

In my opinion, motherhood was over glamorized by the media. There seemed to be a conspiracy to shield the harsh truth about motherhood from young women approaching child bearing age. Especially for working mothers, it was impossible to live up to externally imposed expectations of balancing career and motherhood, while maintaining a romantic marriage. In the 1980's a new surge of advocacy for mothers to breast feed their babies as long as possible added another layer of pressure. My Pediatrician, by the way a male doctor, insisted that I refrain from bottle feeding or using a pacifier that might cause "nipple confusion" for the new born. Feeding the new baby every two hours and each end-to-end feeding process took at least one hour, I felt like a cow, my only purpose was for milking. Honestly, I did not feel the joy of motherhood, and I felt deeply guilty for having those thoughts. I was enveloped in post-partum blues and insecurity while striving to do what was expected of as a good mother. I was clearly unfit as a mother.

I believe a baby is innately in tune with the mother's emotions. My depression probably caused my first born to be a poor sleeper and cry frequently at night, unless she was held and rocked continuously. Weaning off breast and switching to bottle feed is probably the most traumatic event for both mother and baby. After three months of maternity leave, I had to return to work. I introduced bottle feeding for the very first time. Stephanie was a strong willed baby and refused to drink from the bottle. Her little lips clamped shut as soon as the rubber nipple touched her lips. She wailed in protest and hunger. Finally, the pediatrician instructed me to stop breast feeding completely until she accepted drinking from the bottle. It was the worse gut wrenching experience to hear your own baby wailing and still refusing to drink from a bottle for over twenty four hours. Finally she gave in from hunger and pure exhaustion. I was able to leave her with a nanny and go back to work the next day. But, I could not forgive myself for putting my own baby through such a traumatic event in order to resume the career that I seemed to value more than my baby. I believe most working parents struggle with such ambivalence and guilt. We just don't talk about it. Especially Asian American immigrants families. We learned early in life to suck it up, and don't complain.

I learned a big lesson, and determined that my second baby will be proficient with both breast and bottle feeding from day one!

Growing up with ACEs made me over protective and controlling as a parent. While I wanted to provide everything that I was deprived as a child, and definitely be a much better parent than my own, I created a lot of anxiety for myself and Co as new parents. In the process for striving for a better future, I missed the joy of the present moment. However, I was never the stereotyped "Tiger Mom." Raising a child in the Chinese American community of the San Gabriel Valley of Los Angeles, you are expected to produce super stars with excellent academic and artistic performance. Although I did the typical circuit such as baby gym, swimming, piano, ballet, tap dancing, gymnastics, ice skating, painting, and Mandarin Chinese lessons, I never pressured my children to be the number one performer. If they did not show interest, we typically drop the extracurricular activity and moved on to the next. They were always encouraged to be creative and find their own interests. My Asian friends and relatives often implied critically that I was not strict enough, because my girls did not speak Chinese. Even my dear mother-in-law made comments that my children did not know how to speak Chinese, because I did not cook in a wok. I knew she said it jokingly, but those words hurt and further reinforced my insecurity as mother. I never pushed my children to go to ivy league schools as most Asian American parents, but I started to save for their college tuitions since their birth, so they didn't have to work three jobs to put themselves through college as I did.

Unconsciously, I became more like my mother, who enjoyed her career more than the role of mother and house wife. Because the reward for your performance in a successful career was tangible, whereas being a mother, I always felt inadequate. Honestly, I was doing the best I knew how, balancing career and being the perfect Chinese American wife and mother. I resumed working full time and went back to graduate school full time after maternity leave. In hindsight, the biggest challenge for working parents was finding good child care. Sadly, our first child went through nightmare child care arrangements before she reached the pre-school age. We started with a friend's mother as the nanny, but she quit with short notice, because she decided to take care of her new grandbaby instead. We tried home day care by a neighbor one summer, and later found out that she literally placed our baby in the car seat, while she drove her three older children to various sports events and summer swim lessons. My two year old Stephanie was sun burned, dehydrated, and had inconsolable tantrums by the time I picked her up. Then, a good intentioned friend from church introduced a child care arrangement offered by the church pastor and his wife. Naively we thought a child care center ran by the pastors must be trustworthy. Later we found out, it was a religious cult, and they practiced corporal punishment of the young children according to the biblical teaching. Again, I felt like I was failing motherhood and I was losing control. As I was self-consumed and overwhelmed from managing my role as a new working mother, I completely neglected Co, who was also struggling with adjustment and increasing stress from work. Our marriage started to erode. We started to have more arguments. I wanted to take my child and flee at one point. But a little voice within me stopped me. I cannot and will not fail in my marriage as my parents did. Because their divorce caused so much suffering, I refused to repeat the same mistakes and expose my own child to the same trauma. Subsequently, Co and I went through years of counseling to re-set and rebuild our marriage. A union of two persons with separate trauma from ACEs and PTSD, in our case, required years of individual and marriage therapy. The healing journey is never easy, but we never gave up on each other.

Another unexpected consequence of motherhood revealed itself at work. All of a sudden, I could not maintain equanimity taking care of my pediatric patients. I saw my own child's face in every patient, the intense emotion of motherhood seeped through the protective professional boundary. The emotional stress of balancing motherhood, marriage, and the demands of being a nurse taking care of children with catastrophic conditions, took a toll on me. I was tired of having to prioritize my patients over my own child.

"Mommy, can you stay home with me, today? I don't feel good." Stephanie often pleaded with me when she had to stay home due to fever.

" I am so sorry, baby, Mommy has to go to work and take care of kids who are much sicker." I could not believe that was my typical response, when my own child needed me at her side. I always felt obligated to leave her behind, because my patients at the Children's Hospital had cancer and needed more care than common childhood illnesses. I was applying the Nurse Triage process to my own child. What message was I giving to my own child?

The escalating stress from trying to do everything perfectly and failing might have attributed to a miscarriage of my second pregnancy when Stephanie was three years old. At that point, I left bed side nursing and moved into in care management and a quality improvement position, away from direct patient care.

When Stephanie was six years old, I had my second daughter Brittany. This time I learned to be kinder to myself as a mother. I paced myself during pregnancy to enjoy every moment, including a family trip to the beautiful island of Maui, where we enjoyed our time as a family of three. Stephanie and I swam and took long naps every day waiting for the new arrival. Co and I had a date night while Stephanie had a play date with another little girl of her age from Alaska spending time with her grandmother. Although I was in my third trimester, my obstetrician arranged a backup doctor on the island in case my baby decided to come early like my first delivery.

Brittany was born a full term, healthy, and happy baby. She learned to breast feed and bottle feed effortlessly on day one. I did not heed other's expectations or judgments for motherhood this time around. I found a woman pediatrician who was also balancing her career and raising children. Co was happier as a Dad, for he got to feed the baby with a bottle and bond with his new little girl. We asked my mother-in-law to move closer to us, so she can be the primary baby sitter for Brittany when she was an infant. Since my personal experiences of child care nightmares as a working mother, I joined the hospital employee committee advocating for an onsite day care for infants to school age children for the nurses working all three shifts. Prior to the establishment of the onsite day care, the night shift nurses would bring their school aged children to work at night. The children slept on the floor of the conference rooms in the basement of the hospital.

After the morning shift report, the night shift nurses would drop off their children to school, then they would go home to sleep for a few hours before picking up the children, and then prepare for the next shift. The CHLA state of the art day care included private rooms for infant care as well as a space for sleeping cots for the school age children of the night shift nurses. The employer sponsored day care center was completed just in time for Brittany to benefit. We commuted to work together every day. I met Brittany for lunch at the day care center right across the street from the hospital. After reading a book and tucking her in for the afternoon naps, I returned to the office. It was the perfect arrangement. As we experienced nursing shortages, one of the biggest benefits to attract younger generation nurses was to provide twenty four hours of high quality onsite child care. I am forever grateful for CHLA's day care center that prevented my second child from experiencing avoidable trauma of unsafe child care arrangements.

Sadly for working parents, quality child care services, especially for school age children, continue to be a gap. Although I sent both of my children to private schools with decent extracurricular activities, during the summer, it was always a challenge to find educational or sports summer camps with extended child care. We did not have the financial means to send our school age children to private summer camps, such as sports, arts and music immersion programs, with room and board as many wealthy parents could afford. We often patched together YMCA summer camps at the park with Vacation Bible

School camps offered by the church, and spread our vacation days to keep our children occupied and cared for during the summer.

Because, I grew up taking on adult responsibilities at a very young age without the opportunity to be a normal teenager, I was not a very empathetic parent to my children's trials and tribulations through their adolescent years. But at the same time, as parents with our own trauma, we tend to over protect our children from learning from their mistakes. All my siblings grew up with very little guidance from our parents, whenever we encountered challenges, the expectation was to "suck it up" and get over it. To this date, our immigrant parents thought they did a great job, as if the dysfunctional parenting and the abuse were all by design, because we all turn out to be quite successful based on their standards. They proudly retain their bragging rights to this day.

∞ ♥ ∞

As I continued to excel in my career with increasing demands for more travel, my husband's employer went through a major reduction in force. He was out of a job when our daughters were middle school and high school age. Co and I decided that he would be the stay home parent, while I took on a higher paying job to support the family. It was a perfectly logical decision, but it was extremely difficult for Co due to his traditional Chinese upbringing. It was considered a disgrace to be the stay home parent as a male, while your wife assumed the bread winner role. Co was constantly criticized by his father for not having a job outside of the home as a traditional Chinese family man should. Finally the father and son relationship was severed. They never had a chance to amend their relationship when his father died alone in the nursing home due to COVID19.

I lived and travelled away from our Southern California home for over two years during my job with the Federal Receivership. Co and the girls would drive up North to visit me on weekends, or I flew back home during the holidays. Although I was physically apart from my daughters, I had a very strong invisible bond with my daughters energetically. I often get the mother's sixth sense, that I need to reach out to them individually or together. One evening after a long stressful day of visiting the prisons, I was having a typical end of the day debriefing with my colleague. All of a sudden, I felt like someone punched me in my gut. I doubled over in pain, and started to sob uncontrollably. My colleague was shocked, he had never seen me losing my equanimity and composure. He thought I must be going through some intense stress due to our demanding job. I was surprised by my own loss of control, excused myself, and drove back to my apartment. I called home immediately, even though it was very late at night.

" Are you in your apartment and sitting down?" Co asked.

"Yes, I had a horrible day…" I was about to tell him

what happened at work. But paused when the serious tone of his voice alarmed me.

"Brittany had a car accident around seven PM tonight. She was in the car with her girlfriends heading to a birthday party. The birthday girl's parents were driving in a separate car behind them and witnessed the accident. They were hit by a drunken driver. Brittany was sitting in the middle seat and did not have her seat belt on. They were all transported to the emergency room by ambulance. Please come home!" The time of the impact was the exact time when I felt the punch of pain. Brittany had sustained a spinal fracture and laceration of her face on impact. I flew home immediately. I never forgave myself for not being there to protect my baby girl. I am so grateful that Brittany recovered fully after a body brace and a full year of physical therapy. She still has a scar on her lips that gives her character when she smiles. Her serious car accident was a wakeup call for me, motherhood is an honor, I will never again take that privilege for granted or place my career above my family. Since that incident, whenever I sense that mother's intuition in my body, I will reach out and check in with my girls.

Balancing work, child care, and the old fashion expectations of the Chinese immigrant family was the constant unspoken struggle for my generation, sandwiched between the East and the West. The COVID19 pandemic further amplified the strain on the parents who had to balance the demands of working remotely while keeping their family safe from infections, while the boundaries between multiple demands from all fronts blurred. Typically, the women shoulder the most burden to keep the job, family, and children safe. For the immigrant mothers of the lower economic sectors who continued working at the frontline, the toll on the mother intensified multi-fold because the day care safety net offered by the schools was no longer an option during the pandemic.

Some households benefited from the multigenerational support to mitigate the isolation but at the risk of the older generation becoming infected with COVID19 from the younger children. Having the extended family support definitely helped to buffer the mental health toll of the COVID19 pandemic and the escalating racial tensions of the AAPI hate. As many of us lost the elderly members of our families, I thought a lot about my grandparents during the pandemic. Despite the ACEs, I had fond memories of spending time with my grandfather when I was a little girl. Even with Ching-Ma, as the trauma of my ACEs healed over time, the positive memories of her strength of keeping the family together prevailed. I admire her assertiveness in seeking her own happiness as a woman born before her time. Had I learned about the neuroscience and impact of ACEs and my own score decades ago, I would have benefitted from trauma informed therapy and counseling before becoming a mother. Perhaps ACE screenings and tools should be offered as a standard as part of the new pre-natal education programs.

Although I might have limited capacity as the ideal mother due to my own trauma, I no longer felt intense guilt through years of self-compassion practices, transcendental meditations, and yoga. Self-healing is a life journey of daily practices. I am grateful for the valuable lessons I learned from the mothers before me, including the positive and the negative experiences. I hope to be a more compassionate and caring grandmother. I look forward to that day when our resilience is passed on with unconditional love, and we heal the epigenetic harm in bodies of our future generations.

Self-Healing Moment

5 S of Clearing

Whenever you are feeling overwhelmed, practice the yoga version of 5 S, that I adapted from the 5 S of Lean Process Improvement: sort, set in order, shine, standardize, sustain.

- **Slowdown** - slow down your breath, inhale deeply, exhale slowly and smoothly.
- **Simplify** - simplify your focus by looking around you and behind you, find one thing that you might not have noticed before. Notices its color, shape, and texture.
- **Sensing** - sense any sensation in your body, any tightness or constriction?
- **Surrender** - surrender to the sensation without attachment or judgement.
- **Self-Care** - Select one self-care practice that works for you right now. e.g., sit still, meditate, or take a short walk.

20 PRISON AND PURPOSE

∞ ♥ ∞

"A feeling of aversion or attachment towards something is

your clue that there is work to be done."

-Rumi

Feeling blissful meditating on the back porch of my little cottage overlooking the serene backwater of Kerala, India. The cool air still felt damp with the departing night sky, the early birds started chirping with the rising sun, colorful dragon flies were gliding over the surface of the calm water covered with bright pink lotus flowers lazily gazing up at the morning sky. My heart filled with immense gratitude to be here celebrating my sixtieth birthday with my two daughters and my yoga tribe. Between the spread of green lotus leaves, patches of Pontederia crassipes, commonly known as water hyacinth were floating rootless in the open waters with the gentle current, no attachment. Some adorned with beautiful freshly bloomed lavender lily flowers, complementing the majestic bright pink lotus flowers. The water hyacinth is a free floating aquatic plant native to tropical and subtropical climate. Although the fast growing plants can be invasive, in countries like India and Thailand, the water hyacinth's stems are used as braiding materials and sources of fibers to make baskets, furniture and paper. I often thought of the water hyacinth as the metaphor for my wandering life as a child of broken families and an Asian American with immigrant origin, rootless and never belonging. Yet the innate will to thrive with a purpose propelled me forward every day. The beauty of not having a place that you belong in the physical world, forces you to find the point of belonging and grounding from within. Realizing that we are all connected and belonging to each other in this universe was that awakening moment for me.

I became a yoga teacher purely out of desperation to find balance when my life was turned upside down. I stumbled upon yoga at the LA Fitness. Yoga for me was just another form of exercise as a typical non-athletic gym participant. I tried visiting the gym at least once a week. My routine included hopping on the treadmill while watching a sitcom on the screen or listening to pop music mindlessly. After a round of fitness machines, my task was done. A box checked. During the week, I inserted a few fitness classes after work, to break up the boring routine. Yoga classes in most gyms were watered down secular versions of exercises focused on building strength and firming abs. One day we had a substitute yoga teacher. She was different. She started the class sitting, taught us how to root down, turning to the breath, and asked us to set an intention.

I felt a different energy in my first sun salutation, linking movement with breath. She started teaching each pose from the ground up. It was the first yoga class that I stayed in the present moment and my mind did not wander to mundane tasks or worries. I felt safe and grounded. After the long savasana or corpse pose, I felt light as a feather with a feeling of deep calm. I was hooked. I joined a real yoga studio and started practicing with authentic yoga teachers. When I took off my corporate hat, I was on the yoga mat.

∞ ♥ ∞

My life journey taught me that what seemed to be negative, or unexpected turns of events, were really stepping stones on my life journey leading to my true purpose. By embracing the inability to control my environment, I slowly learned to let go and be open to what comes with no judgment or attachment. Often what I perceived as setbacks or failures were the universe's message of telling me to be still, and trust that all good things will come to me at the perfect time with grace and ease for the greater good.

I was laid off at the peak of my career. Health care was in a state of flux, and at the same time, the economy was tanking. I was the only working parent in our household, with two daughters in college and a mortgage to pay. For the first time in my career, I could not find a job. There was so much uncertainty in the health care industry and the stock market, that no company was hiring. I felt my life was turned upside down. That year, as an effort to get my life back in balance, I set a simple goal to find balance upside down literally. Since the only control I had was myself, my body, I decided to redirect my nervous energy to learn how to do a handstand. Doing a handstand was no small feat for a non-athletic half century old person. Since I didn't have a job, and I had plenty of free time on my hands, I signed up for yoga teacher training to learn how to do a handstand properly and safely. I realized the obstacle was really my own fear. My master yoga teacher helped me overcome my fear, I found inner balance, and did my first adho mukha vrksasana, the Sanskrit name for handstand translated literally to upward facing tree. Just like a tree, I learned to root down through my palms with roots extending deep into the earth, then rise up through my core with the strength and power of the tiger. By the time I became an official yoga teacher, the market began to recover. The health care reform bill was in the horizon, and job offers started pouring in.

Yoga helped me find balance in my life holistically. I enjoyed teaching yoga and went on for more advanced training to specialize in yoga techniques for those who have experienced trauma. Teaching yoga held me accountable to my own self-care and to maintain balance personally. I have to first find my own center in order to hold a safe space to teach my students. Not only did I accomplish a personal goal, I found a love for yoga, and its connection to health care. I went on to become certified in teaching Trauma-Informed yoga, which has had a tremendous impact on my volunteer work.

Allow me to rewind at this juncture, and share with you what transpired in my life before the lay-off. My career was taking off after graduate school. I transitioned out of the hospital walls as a clinical nurse into managed care. I developed acumen for start-ups, for example, helping provider groups implement Medi-Cal (California Medicaid) Managed Care contracts and program requirements. I rode the wave of global risk, capitation, mergers and acquisitions in the 1990's; implementing medical management platforms for start-up health plans. At one of the managed care conferences, I realized that in order to impact the health care delivery system, I needed to move up the P-ladder, from provider to payer to policy. I eventually joined the Center for Health Care Strategies; a progressive policy think tank in New Jersey advocating for the managed care model in the state Medicaid programs. I was a telecommuter living in California while travelling frequently to various states. One day, out of the blue, I received a call from Korn Ferry Executive Recruiter asking if I would be interested in a Chief Nurse Executive (CNE) position as part of the Federal Receivership to reform the California State Prison Medical System. I politely declined and explained that my clinical background was in pediatric and quality improvement, I had zero experience in correctional health care. To be honest, not many health care professionals went into medicine or nursing with the goal of working in prisons. The recruiter stated that this opportunity was historically unprecedented, and they were specifically looking for a nurse leader outside of the traditional correctional justice system. The Korn Ferry recruiter perked my interest, I decided to do some research on my own.

Not many people connected the War on Drugs as the systemic strategy designed by the US government to legitimize the mass incarceration of people of color in this country. I did not connect the two dots until I researched about the history leading up to the Receivership. Later, Michelle Alexander's book, The New Jim Crow, published in 2010, provided an extraordinary detailed account of systemic racism by design in the US. Drug offenses accounted for over half of the rising prison population between 1985 to 2000. The situation was exacerbated with the popular tough on crime law, such as the three strikes law in California. The overcrowding in the California state prisons attributed to California Department of Correction and Rehabilitation (CDCR) failing Eighth Amendment standards proscribing cruel and unusual punishment. The lack of access to timely medical care caused preventable prisoner deaths in CDCR at the rate of 64 per year by 2005 despite multiple class action law suits in the past 25 years. In 2006, Senior U.S. District Court Judge Thelton E. Henderson ordered an unprecedented mandate stripping away the $1.2 billion CDCR healthcare authority and appointed highly acclaimed health administrator Robert Sillen, as the Receiver to take over control effective April 17, 2006.

After several interviews including a very intense panel of militant CDCR leadership, I was offered the job by the Receiver that I could not say no. Deep within my being, I knew this was the path that I must embark upon tapping into the strength and courage of the tiger. Even though I had never step foot into the prison. The job required me to leave my husband and two daughters in Southern California. My husband was committed to be the stay home parent while I work away from home for the next five years per the original contract. We were committed for a cause greater than our selves.

∞ ♥ ∞

I was the first AAPI in such leadership position in the state prison system. I learned later that words spread quickly in the prisons that the Receiver hired a pediatric nurse as the Statewide Chief Nurse Executive and Chief Clinical Turnaround Officer responsible for restoring constitutional rights of the adult prisons. Many joked about it and doubted my ability to take up such a daunting challenge. I leaned on my experience as organizational change agent, and I seek first to understand with humility and none-judgement. I showed up at the California Men Colony (CMC) with the Receiver on the first day of the job. My first impression of CMS was a surprise, it did not look ominous like any prison I saw on the television. It was more like a modest country club located in a green valley with pleasant Pacific ocean breeze, with the exception of the bar wire fences enclosure. In fact, CMC has been called the "Country Club" among the California prisons for its wide variety of vocational training, academic, and mental health treatment programs. Subsequently, I learned from the Correctional Officers that CMC was a preferred prison for law enforcement or correctional professionals who committed crimes. They would likely be killed or harmed by the general population of other prisons dominated by people of color. Hence, CMC was considered a safer prison for certain inmates. Also I learned quickly that CMC was the only prison without a problem recruiting physicians, for CMC is located in the beautiful San Luis Obispo, a city in the California Central Coast region, well known by tourist for its lively downtown, restaurants, historic Spanish mission, museums and art galleries. A perfect place for physicians to retire with an ocean view property and work in the well-staffed CMC, full time or part time.

On the second day, I met all the wardens at their annual meeting and introduced myself. By showing respect first, I earned their respect which was a very important core value according to former correctional professionals and the inmates. The rumor spread quickly that after the first week on the job, "The new CNE may be small in stature, but she is not afraid to stand toe to toe with the wardens."

The state prisons were very much segregated by race, gender preference, disabilities, types of crime, and gang affiliations within its walls. The structural oppression was by design and legitimized by the correctional punitive culture. It was a world that I would never have stepped into if not for this role. But once you see the injustices and the inhumane treatment of human beings in your own back yard, you can never turn your eyes away.

San Quentin is a majestic old architecture sitting on the prime ocean front property over-looking the San Francisco Bay's glistening sapphire blue ocean. The most beautiful location in the bay area for 7000 inmates including the lifers, the facility was built for a maximum capacity of 4000 inmates. The main gate of the prison opened into a court yard to the right and a circular memorial to the left. Each stone of the memorial marked with the name of a custody officer and the day he or she was killed on duty at San Quentin. Despite the pristine ocean air and beautiful surroundings, you are reminded of the seriousness of this place and its ominous history. San

Quentin was surprisingly relaxed with its security compared to the more modern prisons such as High Desert. Inmates in bright orange color or blue denim uniforms walked around freely. Occasionally you see lifers, or condemned inmates in white jumpsuits, with chain cuffs on wrists and waist, accompanied by armed custody officers being transported across the yard.

By that time, I was known in the prisons for doing the Gemba walks, which is the action of going to see the actual process, understand the work, and ask questions, and learn. Gemba walk is a fundamental part of Lean management philosophy. I was probably the first and only Chief ever requested to walk with the frontline nursing staff and experience what they do in the prison, and observe how they care for patients behind bars.

My first observation was the medication administration process in the C-Block Adjustment Unit, a place for inmates with behavior problems that needed to be "adjusted." I had to put on a heavy stab vest as precaution before entering the unit. Each inmate was locked in the solitary confinement within the cell enclosed by four iron walls about the size of a closet. Some cell walls were padded to prevent inmates from self-harm or suicide. A sally port secured opening the size of a small shoe box, was located at the cell door for passing of food or medications. Can you image the nurse obtaining blood pressure of the patient through the sally port? One inmate had a sign next to the cell door: "Three guards required for extraction."

"This inmate is a lifer. His objective in life is to kill one of us." Accordingly to the custody officer next to me. He also instructed me to stand away from the open sally port and the creases between the locks and the cell door.

" The inmates here will shoot excrements or spit out of these openings. So be careful." I cannot fathom the desperation of a human being pushed beyond the limit of a caged animal existence. Many of these inmates started with mental illness requiring treatment instead of incarceration and punishment. Once they are locked up in the Adjustment Unit, it is a miracle to ever recover. Despite the extreme caution for security and safety, I was surprised to see the nurse handing a syringe with needle and a bottle of insulin to the inmate through the sally port, and instructed him to draw up his own insulin and inject the medication. The nurse told me they want to teach the inmates self-care as they were taught in nursing school. I was thinking, does she realize these inmates would never be free until they die in the prison?

My heart felt constricted, and the stab vest weighed heavier and heavier as I learned about each inmate locked in the C-Block. A ragged looking inmate, even under the unshaven face, I could tell he was a young man. He turned his head and lowered his gaze as we arrived in front of his sally port.

"This inmate never trusts anyone and he does not

like to look at you. He only speaks to two officers." The correctional officer explained.

As the nurse offered his medication, I swore I heard him whispered "Thank you." I stood in front to his cell as the other moved to the next cell. For a brief moment, he looked up, I looked at him in the eyes and greeted him with a nod, and he smiled. It was not a menacing type of smile, but a smile that yearned to connect with a kind soul.

After removing the heavy stab vest, I carried the heaviness of the C-Block experience with me forever. Moving on was the East Block, a five story of prison cells stacked on top of each other. Each cell housed two inmates. There were approximately 500 inmates, mostly black-bodies. These inmates came from the reception area and were waiting to be moved to a more permanent unit or transferred to other prisons. There were only two correctional officers on duty.

I followed the two nurses on duty, the more experienced nurse was orienting a new nurse. They both looked young, probably a year or two older than my own daughters. They had to administer insulin to a line of inmates on the ground level before breakfast. The nurses had to administer medication cell by cell up the five story East Block with no custody escort. It was a surreal experience walking up the metal ramps giving medication cell by cell with caged human beings pacing in spaces smaller than the cells for Zoo animals.

I heard heart wrenching story after story as I visited each prison, and I personally witnessed the inhumane treatment of persons with chronic medical conditions, physical disabilities, and mental illnesses. Due to the prison overcrowding situation, many prisons created makeshift confinement spaces in the gyms with tripled bunked beds for the general population. Many young men who sustained gun-shot wounds often required wheel chairs, but there was no consideration of their physical disability with the bunk assignment. For those with serious medical conditions requiring assistance, they were often placed in solitary confinement at the medical unit by default.

The Receiver's Chief Medical Officer, Dr. Terry Hill, and I made a routine of interviewing two to three inmates with medical conditions during our visit at each state prison. It was important to hear their stories in their voices. I met Mr. D, a forty-six year old black male diagnosed with Amyotrophic Lateral Sclerosis (ALS) or commonly known as the Lou Gehrig's disease. ALS is a progressive nervous system disease that eventually causes loss of muscle controls. Because of his diagnosis, Mr. D was initially assigned the California Medical Facility (CMF) of Vacaville, a prison with medical mission. But he was quickly transferred to High Desert State Prion (HDSP), simply because he was a "three-striker" despite the fact that his third strike was a non-violent crime according to Mr. D. HDSP is a modern prison complex designed with high security in mind to prevent escape. The gray building made of concrete and steel surrounded by 364 miles of electrical wires and chain link fencing in the middle of the desert near the Nevada state border. He was placed in an isolation room in the Correctional Treatment Center (CTC) of the HDSP which was designed for inmates with physical disabilities and orthopedic conditions from trauma. By the time of the transfer, Mr. D was already experiencing increasing respiratory paralysis with slurred speech as he struggled to tell his story. Since he lost the use of his right arm and hand due to deterioration of his condition, Mr. D required assistance to get out of bed. He was confined in the isolation room around the clock as if he was in administrative confinement for punishment. He should be in a long term care facility instead.

When we met Mr. D, he was sitting in a padded chair, in a food stained old sweat shirt and pajama pants, staring at a poorly focused television screen fuzzy with snowflakes. Under administrative isolation, the inmate was entitled to be out of the isolation room two hours per day.

"If I am lucky, someone will get me out of this room two or three times per week. I know I am going to die soon, I am asking for a compassionate release, so I can see my family and die with some dignity." Mr. D continued to write letters from the inside with the help of an advocate; while his family appealed from the outside for a compassionate release. I felt my eyes welling up with tears to see a fellow human being wasted away in the prison, suffering from physical, emotional, and mental pain, because of the three strike law. It took another six months of appeal, before Mr. D was transferred to hospice at CMF and reunited with his family before he passed.

∞ ♥ ∞

One of the rare highlights of the Receiver's prison tour was the visit to the CalFire Ishi Fire Crew preparedness drill held at the Ishi Conservation Camp. CalFire Ishi Fire Crew is a model training program of collaboration between the state agencies, the California Department of the Forestry and Fire Protection (CalFire), CDCR, and the Division of the Juvenile Justice. Inmates are trained as fire fighters to help with all types of fire emergencies including the massive forest fires in California. The annual fire crew exercise provides an opportunity for the inmate fire crew to be evaluated on safety performance, physical conditioning, and firefighting knowledge. The inmates who were participating in the 22nd Annual Fire Crew Exercise were very excited knowing the Federal Receiver team will be observing their performance.

As the doctor and nurse leaders of the Receiver team, Dr. Terry Hill and I often travelled together visiting state prisons built in the most remote and undesirable locations. The road trip to Ishi Camp, through the land where the people of Yahi and Yana once lived, was one of the most treacherous road trips yet surrounded by stunning nature. We literally drove through four seasons in one day, from blazing sun, heavy rainstorm, to fresh snow at the peak of the mountain. At the time, I did not have the contemplative awareness or practice to pulse, and appreciate the breathtaking beauty all around in that moment.

I would have never learned about the Native American Yahi Indians and the California genocide by the settlers, had I not visited the Ishi Camp. The Camp was name after Ishi, who was the last survivor of the Yahi tribe. He escaped the genocide and hid most of his life isolated from modern American society. He emerged in 1911, at the age of 50, twenty years after his tribe was wiped out. Ishi was acclaimed as the "last wild Indian" and is studied as a novelty in academic settings and in films. He actually had a real name by birth, but he could not speak his own name until formally introduced by another Yahi according to his culture. Sadly, the California genocide of the Native Americans including the Yahi people, kept him forever silenced to speak his name. Ishi, meaning "man" in the Yahi language, was a name given to him by an anthropologist from the University of California at Berkley. Ironically, the prison inmates, a marginalized population, are trained at a camp shrouded with the history of horrendous trauma of the Native Americans.

During the annual fire crew exercise, I had the opportunity of following the inmates to the fire simulation site in the natural rugged terrain, where they could demonstrate all the skills learned with precision. As the young men lined up at the conclusion of the exercise they were covered with ashes, sweaty, tired, but beamed with pride for their accomplishments. After the exercise, the inmates working in the kitchen prepared delicious BBQ chuck roast for the guests to celebrate their peers. The fire camp program offered a well-rounded occupational training opportunity for the inmates. Tragically, the institutional structure in the free world would not allow them to use the job skills they had learned while in prison.

It is not widely known by the public that California continued to rely on more than 1000 inmates to help fight the state's destructive wildfires every year. The inmates at the fire camp program are only paid $1 to $2 an hour in camp, and they earn an additional $1 to $2 when deployed to fight wild fires. According to CDCR, the prison fire camp program saves the California tax payers approximately $100 million annually. I finally understood the economic benefit of the New Jim Crow in the prison system. The inmate firefighters were trained and deployed to the most dangerous zone to fight fires during the wildfire season. Yet, when they are released from the prisons, these proud young men and women will never be hired as full time fire fighter per Federal Judge's decision. I took mental notes, and was more determined to find ways to prevent young people from entering the prison system.

∞ ♥ ∞

Despite the massive attempt to reform the state prison health care system, it was very clear to me that the state prisons system have become the default mental health institutions, especially for people of color. Based on the Prison Legal News report in 2020, approximately 40% of the prisoners in the US have a mental health diagnosis. 14% of them suffer from serious mental illness with higher risk for suicide. California state prisons have the highest suicide rate, followed by the Federal Bureau of Prisons, and the Texas Department of Criminal Justices.

The cost to remediate the state prison problems and restore the constitutional rights of the incarcerated population became cost prohibitive and unacceptable by the state legislators, when the cost per prisoner was more than the cost of higher education per student. The original Receiver team established a health care organization structure including implementation of pharmacy and medical management systems, and changing the state law mandating CDCR hire qualified Chief Executive Appointment (CEA) positions. The new law prevented career civil services CEA's to assume the health care leadership positions by seniority and with no health care experience. The new law required hiring health care CEA's based on health care core competencies and performance. The CNE position was the first to be established under the new law followed by health care CEO and CMO. Most importantly, the reformed organization structure ensured the health care employees report to the health care CEO chain of command, not to the warden, in order to up hold the Do No Harm culture in the prisons. The person who "adjusts" or punishes the inmate can never be the same person who treats them or literally stitch them up. The physicians who worked under the health care organization of the prisons were forbidden to write the lethal injection order to put an inmate to death.

Unfortunately, the political landscape shifted in California due to economic down turn before the end date of our contract. After the Receiver was replaced by a state appointed civil services employee, Dr. Terry Hill and I were laid off few months later. But, I am proud to say that we have successfully implemented our succession plan, trained enough mission-focused physician and nurse leaders to lead the new health care organization, and continue to spread the Do No Harm culture in all 33 state prisons. My job in the prison ended. But I saw enough to be committed to stop the school-to-prison pipe line in my community. I finally understood why a pediatric nurse was selected to help reform the adult prisons. As the witness of inhumane treatment of people of color and the systemic racial injustice within the prison walls, my purpose just begun to be revealed.

My life is a personal testimony of the verse in the book of Ecclesiastes, "...there is a time for everything, and a season for every activity under heaven." I do believe that events and people come into your life for a reason. We might not have control over what happened to us, but we sure can change our mind set and lean into the unknown with curiosity. After the detour of my career into the dark pit of the health care delivery system in the state prison system, yoga helped me find balance, and finally return back to a successful health care career in the "free" world. But the faces of the young people, who absolutely did not belong in the state prisons, haunted me.

∞ ♥ ∞

As I start to honor my own need to be still and practice self-care daily without guilt, my mind became clearer, I started to see how events connect in my life for a greater purpose. Instead of obsessing with planning and controlling everything, I am finally cultivating enough courage to embrace the unknown with grace and ease. I am learning to trust that the right path will reveal itself, and the right door will open at the perfect timing. Right after I completed the 500 hour professional yoga teacher's training specialized in trauma informed yoga, I ran into my colleague, Dr. Cristina Jose-Kampfner, a clinical psychologist, whom I had not seen since we worked together previously. Dr. Jose-Kampfner was the founder of the 360 Turnaround Youth Diversion program, a non-profit organization in Santa Ana, California.

When she was working as the clinical psychologist in the Orange County juvenile detention center, she realized the majority of the incarcerated youth were Hispanic from one zip code in the city of Santa Ana. She decided to intervene up stream with a targeted program within that one zip code. With the start-up support of the local Catholic church, she created the 360 Turnaround Youth Diversion program for the first offender youth in the midst of the housing projects, in the part of the city known for the highest crime rate and drug trafficking. The program empowered parents by offering them the parenting skills to help building resiliency in the high risk youth; while resourcing the youth with self-regulation skills to grow into healthy productive members of the communities. Since 360 Turnaround Youth Diversion opened in 2013, crime rate has gone down dramatically in the neighborhoods served, and school performance for youth who participate has steadily and dramatically improved.

The mission of 360 Turnaround Youth Diversion was to prevent high risk youth from entering the criminal justice system and reduce the incarceration rate among youth in Orange County, California. The holistic diversion program included cognitive behavioral therapy (CBT), mindfulness meditation, trauma informed yoga practice, and organic urban gardening. The 360 Turnaround Youth Diversion Program aimed to empower parents and youth to initiate positive change in their lives by influencing value development through positive alternatives.

" It is so difficult to find a volunteer yoga teacher who is willing to work with these difficult kids." Dr. Jose-Kampfner commented as she told me about her program.

" Well, Cristina, timing seems to be perfect. I just received my yoga teacher certification, and I specialized in teaching yoga with a trauma informed approach. I would like to volunteer at the 360 Youth Diversion Program." I shared my prison health care reform story and my desire to help stop the incarceration of children. Stopping the school-to-prison pipeline in high risk communities became my mission on the yoga mat.

Since a yoga mat is considered a luxury item for the kids from the low income household, I wrote a proposal to Jade Yoga corporation, and they generously donated twelve yoga mats. Teaching trauma informed yoga to adolescents is very different from teaching average adults in the yoga studio. Although I always came prepared with the yoga theme to coincide with Dr. Jose-Kampfner's cognitive behavioral therapy focus of the day, I had to be prepared to change my teaching based on the teen's emotional and physical state of the moment. My job as the trauma informed yoga teacher was to create a safe place for them to learn self-regulation through yoga and to take these tools with them off the yoga mat. For example, we always started the class with a mindful check in, the interoception practices helped these adolescents sense their own feeling and name it. Many of the adolescents got into trouble at school or on the street, because they had difficulty controlling outbursts of anger. Fights involved drugs and weapons and led to the arrests by the police. The check in practice helped them to sense their own emotions and bring to a conscious level by naming it. We incorporated organic gardening activities as part of the proprioception practice of tactile feeling of their body in nature as simple as touching the earth and feeling the rich soil with bare hands. Once the teens learned how to grow vegetables and fruits trees in the organic garden, and felt safe in the yoga classes, we started offering self-regulation tools that thy could take with them. Once, I asked them to select a branch from their fruit tree in the shape of a small stick to bring to yoga class. We were learning cognitive acronyms tools, such as "S.T.I.C." that I adapted from Dr. Sam Himelstein's Mindfulness based Substance Abuse Treatment for Adolescents curriculum. "S" stands for Stop, "T" stands for Take a deep breath, "I" stands for Imagine the future consequences; "C" stands for Choose wisely. Learning to access breath was a big part of the trauma informed yoga practice, so that the adolescents could experience what relaxation felt like in a safe place. By the way, I never used the word "relax" in the trauma informed yoga class, because the word could be a trigger for teens who experienced sexual violence. It was interesting to observe that some of the participants fell into deep sleep during savasana even snoring loudly. I later learned from the promotora, community worker, that many of them lived in a neighborhood or household with violence or loud noises that they can never rest. The safe yoga space was the only place they felt safe to sleep. Eventually, all the students learned to hold the sacred space to allow fellow students to wake up naturally after savasana, even when the class was officially over. Although the program was in place before ACEs screening became a standard of care, I suspect all the adolescents participated in the program had four or more ACEs. In the first three years, the 360 Youth Diversion Program maintained a zero recidivism rate. Whenever the graduating adolescent returned as volunteers, we knew the program was making a positive impact. One of the returning older boys told me that he carried his STIC everywhere as a reminder to breathe.

In addition to offering the ten week program, the 360 Youth Diversion Program also raised funds to help the family pay the restitution fines, so the adolescent could participate in the program and avoid incarceration. I started a donation based Wellness Yoga in the Park in my neighborhood, where 100% of the proceeds were donated directly to the 360 Youth Diversion program to pay for the restitution fee, yoga equipment, and hire regular yoga teachers for the after school program for the younger children. As the Juvenile detention center's census was steadily dropping to below the state and national average, the program came to halt with the start of the COVID19 pandemic.

I am very hopeful that programs such as 360 Youth Diversion offering buffering support, will be adapted into the mainstream health care system with appropriate funding stream alignment. I am grateful for the leadership of physician champion like Dr. Nadine Burke Harris, California's first Surgeon General, the neuroscientific evidence of trauma informed early intervention to reverse the harm of the ACEs is being widely recognized and promoted in the primary care delivery system. I personally believe healing the trauma deep within our body with self-compassion and self-regulation is a necessary first step to dismantling systemic racism and to achieving racial health equity.

Self-Healing Moment

Honoring the Self

- Start your day with a moment dedicating to yourself. Because every human being wants to be heard, be accepted, be validated, and be loved, so let us start with the self.
- Find a quiet place to sit.
- Feel your seat connecting with the earth supporting you, as you feel the energy rising up through your spine toward the crown of your head.
- Connect with your breaths.
- Tell you self, "I am here for you…"
- Breathe in and breathe out in stillness.
- Notice whatever sensations or thoughts rise up, with no judgement, simply tell yourself " I hear you…, I feel you."
- Let it be.
- Continue to breathe in and breathe out until you are ready to start your day.
- End your practice with saying to yourself: "I love you. I love you. I love you."

21 RESILIENCE

∞ ♥ ∞

"At the year's turn,

in the days between,

we step away

from what we know

Into spaces

We cannot yet name.

Slowly the edges

begin to yield,

the hard places

soften,

the gate of forgiveness

opens."

-Marcia Falk

Everything happens at the perfect time for a purpose. I woke at dawn with unusual pressure and pain in my lower abdomen. The pain intensified by the minute. A nurse by training, I knew this was not normal.

"Honey, wake up. My stomach is hurting really bad. I think I need to go to urgent care as soon as it opens to have it checked," I whispered to my sleeping husband, Steve.

"It must be food poisoning. It will pass." He rolled over and continued to sleep.

"I had a late lunch and early dinner yesterday. There is nothing in my stomach." I felt the pain spreading through my entire abdomen below the navel. Then I started vomiting. Steve then looked at my face wincing with pain, and he knew it was serious at first glance, because I hardly ever get sick. He took me to the nearest Kaiser urgent care, which was only five miles away, but it took forever because of California's infamous rush hour traffic on the 405 freeway. After checking in, I had to be taken to the urgent care unit by wheel chair. I could not walk with the increasing pain in my abdomen. Since I had to keep my face mask on, I felt like I was suffocating as I retched. A familiar sense of panic welled up inside me.

I was placed in treatment room 11 to wait alone due to COVID19 precautions. As soon as the doctor entered, I asked for some pain medication.

"Sorry Ms. Ha, we cannot give you anything right now. We don't want to mask the pain until we find out what is causing it," the doctor said behind her N95 mask. I could see her kind and sympathetic eyes. I started to retch and vomit again as she was preparing the physical exam. "How about we give you some medicine to ease the nausea? The nurse can draw some blood for the lab at the same time. I will come back to examine you when the medication takes effect."

"Thank you, doctor." I leaned back in the exam chair as the pain continued to intensify while waves of nausea pulled me down into a deep ocean of misery. The nurse finally came, drew my blood for the lab, and started a port for intravenous medication. The retching stopped shortly, and the doctor examined me and ordered a computed tomography scan to rule out kidney stones. As I waited for my name to be called in the imaging waiting area, I took note of my experience as a helpless patient: minutes waiting felt like an eternity since I was in severe pain. By the time the scan was complete, the effect of the antiemetic medication had worn off. I started to vomit more profusely in the waiting area. The urgent care nurse quickly took me to the treatment room, started intravenous hydration, and immediately gave me more antiemetics followed by my first dose of pain medication. By now, the pain felt like labor contractions for birth, but without the break between contractions. Suddenly, I felt a familiar pain in my right side, behind my right kidney. The pain suddenly triggered a memory of me as a ten year old child suffering from pediatric kidney disease, experiencing the same intensity of pain that I had long forgotten. I saw myself as a child lying on a bamboo rattan recliner chair under the bamboo trellis covered in grapevines, the sunlight peeping through the jade green leaves like beams of diamonds. The child was left all alone. The pain felt was much deeper, reaching into the pit of my soul. The pure pain of that memory - the abandoned child - finally surfaced, as I was lying there on the stretcher with intravenous fluid dripping into my body like a new life force. The vivid memory emotionally overwhelmed me at that moment of vulnerability.

"Lean in, my dear," I heard my inner voice saying: "Embrace this opportunity. Allow the soul-pain to be purged along with the physical pain you are experiencing right now. It is all good. Use the same trauma-informed yoga resources as you teach others: somatic experiencing, inner awareness, proprioception."

I looked around the treatment room and noticed the sign "Keep Your Mask on at All Times!" I saw the clear normal saline bag hung up high and dripping into my veins. The afternoon sunlight was peeping through the palm leaf-print of the curtain, providing privacy for patients between the treatment rooms. I felt the surface of the gurney supporting me and the sensation of being enveloped by warm heated blankets that the thoughtful and kindhearted nurse placed over me. I felt safe but a deep sadness welled up in me as warm tears rolled down my face. I inhaled deeply: one, two, three, four, paused at the top for four, three, two, one I exhaled one, two, three, four, and held for four, three, two, one. I felt my belly rising and softening with each breath. I felt the pain easing as the medications took effect.

"Hello Ms. Ha, I am your doctor for the new shift." I looked up and greeted my new doctor with a more relaxed gaze. "You look a lot more comfortable now," she said.

"I heard you retching in the hall way earlier. The CT scan confirmed your diagnosis of kidney stones. It is five millimeter in diameter, small enough to pass naturally, so no surgical intervention is required. But I will refer you to a urologist for follow-up. The lab results are mostly normal with a few exceptions. We will email the results to you and the nurse will come in shortly with your discharge orders. Take good care of yourself." I am a petite Asian woman, and imagining a pebble passing through my body was still unfathomable to me. The new charge nurse came back with the discharge orders.

"How long will this pain last?" I asked as she discontinued my IV gently.

"As soon as the stone passes, it will stop, just like turning off a light switch. Then people will ask you, was it a boy or girl?" I could see her eyes smiling and imagined her friendly smile behind her mask. I really appreciated the nurse's way of explaining things and the way she made me feel at ease. The stone finally passed through my body and metaphorically purged the remaining childhood trauma along with the clean pain of my hidden childhood memory.

Every morning, after my daily twenty minute transcendental meditation practice, I start the day by finding a quiet spot in my backyard, a place where I can reflect with deep gratitude. I take a few deep cleansing breaths, allow my body to soften, and feel the earth beneath my feet. I look around me and behind me. I notice the beautiful clear blue sky. I see the busy bees hovering over the purple rosemary flowers and the white Stephanotis flowers blooming towards the sun. Closing my eyes, I hear the finches chirping and the hummingbird's wings buzzing; I feel calm as my body gradually settles into the present moment.

My healing journey requires a daily discipline, one breath at a time, like someone recovering from addictive disorders. Memories of the past will still pop into my mind. Now I can feel and discern what is happening to my body

- the tightness of my chest, surge of angry energy in my gut, or numbness in my hand. Once I recognize "it" is here again, instead of resisting, I allow it to be there with full acceptance with no more attachment. "Why are you here today?" I investigate with curiosity. I breathe and nurture myself with love and compassion. "I am safe and I am free now." The never ending healing journey continues after the book ends.

I am writing the last chapter of this book as Rosh Hashanah begins. I resonate with its message of celebrating the creation of the world; everything can be made new again this day forward. Our book is written by the choices we make moment by moment. Although many of the earlier chapters may be written by our ancestors, grandparents, parents, siblings, or even those who harmed us, we can always choose to re-tell the story, editing the areas that we want to amplify or parts that we choose to leave behind.

My book started with the Paper Tiger, a passive image of wealth, stature, comfort, and fragility of the era. Paper Tiger is a term that refers to someone who appears to be powerful, but is actually ineffectual and unable to withstand challenge. Ironically, it was the spirit of the tiger in the form of the tigress that shaped my life story and instilled resilience in me. In the Chinese culture, the tiger represents the greatest earthly power, the king of all animals. The tiger is revered as one of the four super-intelligent creatures, along with the dragon, phoenix, and tortoise. The Chinese zodiac sign of the tiger is a symbol of indomitable fortitude and bravery. The essence of the tiger spirit also includes strength, cunning, confidence, independence, and protection. In the old Chinese tradition, women often place paper images of the tiger in their homes to keep away rats and snakes and protect their homes from family quarrels and harm. Unfortunately, my grandmother of the Chinese zodiac sign tiger, caused great harm instead of protecting her household. And my mother, the Paper Tiger's daughter, failed to protect her young daughters, despite her failings as a mother, she did open a path to a better future in America for the Paper Tiger's offspring. All of the tigers in this book have passed, but their essence lives in us.

At age of sixty, my mother eventually remarried her first love, my father, after he abandoned his second marriage and children again. He continued to struggle with alcoholism until late seventies when he developed diabetes and other chronic conditions. They retired in Florida - a fresh start for both of them. They founded a nonprofit organization, Evergreen Asian American Senior Club, which served the Asian American senior community in Central Florida. They encouraged all their retired friends from college, many having immigrated to the US, to retire in Orlando, Florida. My father served as the founder president and my mother as the Chief Financial Officer. Although they both have alienated their children from both marriages, their senior social club has flourished. They created their own social support network and new identities apart from their broken families and history of trauma.

They are happy being popular and active in the community that they started. In the new community, they are respected locally for promoting a sense of belonging for Asian Americans, both mid-career professionals and retirees in Central Florida. My father published and edited a local newsletter in Chinese and my mother kept herself busy with fundraising events and networking with small businesses owned by Asian Americans. I must admit that it was quite a surreal experience to find a video of my own mother line dancing on YouTube. Elsie was very proud to be the oldest dancer of the Evergreen Line Dancing Club, which performed at many other senior centers. They filled the vacuum of family alienation with holiday potlucks, parties for various Chinese holidays, and community events, as if they were trying to reinvent the social life of old Shanghai. Other than the grandchildren from me and my biological sister, they have never met the grandchildren from my half-sisters from the Japanese side of the family. All my half-sisters have chosen to protect their children from meeting the father who abandoned their mother and risk exposing them to generational toxicity. Ironically, the situation was reversed from the days when my father married their mother and abandoned his first wife; now he abandoned his second wife and remarried his first wife. Since my parents were never close to their children growing up, they were content just having each other and being together again. But they have caused so much damage in the trails they left behind.

∞ ♥ ∞

During the writing of this book, my mother is already in her late eighties. She is still in good health and living independently with my father. She plays Mahjong with her friends weekly and takes care of my father who has developed multiple health conditions. I speak with her weekly by phone or Face Time. She looks forward to our chats and takes extra effort to look her best for our calls. She always wears make-up on her wrinkle-free face with her smiling lips painted red. In her colorful tailor-fit shirt with matching necklace and earrings, she looks like she is ready to meet her Mahjong friends. This was how she was raised: always look your best! We talk for hours about her happy memories growing up in Shanghai, current politics, her concerns about COVID-19, my father's failing health, and catch up on all of the doctor visits. I often help her make a list of questions for my father's next doctor visit. I am starting to notice her repeating the same stories more frequently. Secretly, I hope I will look as good and feel as lively when I turn eighty!

After years of different therapies and practicing self-care, I have forgiven my parents and my grandparents. I developed a deep compassion for them as frail human beings. I started to record her stories and tried to understand her perspective. Whenever I disclose the painful side of my story that coincided with her absence in that time of my life, she says, "That was awful. I did not know. No one told me." Not knowing or not remembering is her protective armor for survival without remorse. I asked her why she remarried my father, who broke her heart, betrayed her so many times, and caused so much harm to her children. She told me that she felt pity for my father. She believed deeply in her heart that it was their destiny to grow old together. They shared the same war experience, grew up in Shanghai, spoke the same dialect, fell in love with each other, and embarked on separate yet similar immigrant journeys. Their familiar bond was the anchor of belonging that her soul craved to feel settled.

She often chuckled in that bubbly laugh that I became familiar with as an adult.

"You know when you get old, it is nice to have a 老伴 Lau-Ban (old partner), who speaks your language and comes from the same background. All my girlfriends envy us. Mama 想的開 shung-da-kai (open minded)." She merrily mixed English, Mandarin and Shanghainese in our phone conversations.

∞ ♥ ∞

Now I understood the source of my mother's resilience: acceptance, forgiveness, compassion, and be happy with no regrets or guilt from the past. She learned to live in the moment. Or perhaps refusing to process her trauma was a form of self-preservation. Regardless of how she coped, I love my mother for who she is. The Paper Tiger's daughter's legacy is part of me.

I hope my book reveals a common thread of resilience and offers tangible self-care resources for the next generation. We all have a number. You can be conscious or unconscious of any adverse childhood experiences or your ancestors' trauma, but our body keeps the score. Our scars can be hidden deeply within our soul-body. Regardless of the color of your body, the intersectionality of race, gender, and generational trauma are real. Our past unconsciously shaped our choices and actions in the present. My story also provides a glimpse of the complexities of multigenerational trauma through two Chang families, revealing the power imbalance between sons and daughters, the convergence of diverse immigrant experiences, and the compounded epigenetic harms that we have unintentionally passed on to the next generations. I learned to respect the paths my generation chose for self-healing. Once we acknowledge our past with acceptance and forgiveness, given the wisdom and neuroscience-based resources we have today, we can start to change the epigenetics of our future generations and rise up in the full essence of the tiger.

Self-Healing Moment

Affirmation Savasana

- Find a quiet and comfortable place or use a yoga mat for lying down in corpse pose.
- Close your eyes, if you choose.
- Find a sense of grounding by connecting your back body with the surface beneath you.
- Allow the earth energy to support you effortlessly.
- Connect with your normal breaths.
- Scan your body with each breath cycle.
- Use your breaths to soften your body from the crown of the head to the sole of the feet.
- Notice any tightness or discomfort in your body with no attachment or judgement.
- Direct your breaths to parts of your body requiring extra tender loving care.
- When you feel ready, place right hand under the left arm pit with base palm and thumb resting over your heart.
- Place left hand over the right upper arm.
- Feel the gentle hugs created by your arms.
- Imagine you are in a safe container.
- Repeat the following self-affirmation: (You can create your own affirmation or you can record

the following affirmation with your own voice
and play back during this practice)

- o   I am well and happy.
- o   I am healthy and strong.
- o   I am safe and protected.
- o   I am peaceful and at ease.
- o   I am beautiful, bountiful, and blissful.
- Release your arms to rest along the side body,
  palms open, and enjoy your savasana as long as
  you wish.

22 EPILOGUE

∞ ♥ ∞

Writing this book was a very difficult and challenging journey. Many memories that I kept hidden for decades resurfaced, and I had to re-live the trauma and pain. For some family members reading my memoir may be shocked with disbelief to learn about some situations for the very first time. Please take a deep breath and notice the reaction in your body with compassion and no judgement. This is my story and my experience. I felt compelled to reveal family secrets and expose my own deep soul wounds from my perspective. To start the healing process for myself and the next generation is more important than saving face by holding on to the veil of secrecy and denial. We inherited many epigenetic harms from our ancestors, and we all grew up in households with limited capacity for unconditional love. I did the best I knew how as a parent with my own limited capacity to be loving and nurturing. I ask my children's forgiveness for my share of damage to you unintentionally. And I am sorry for not being there when you needed my loving presence the most in your life. As I heal my-self, I open the flood gate of boundless love for my children and grandchildren. The shaming has to stop with my generation.

I am deeply grateful that I am not alone on this healing journey. I always felt the invisible presence intervening and protecting me at the darkest point of my journey; or a kind soul reaching out and pulling me away from the edge of self-destruction and death. I am blessed with my sisters who share the same adverse childhood experiences with different intensity. We all survived with resilience and renewed hope for the future regardless of our own ACE number stories. I am grateful for the ACE screening as a new standard of health care initiated by California Office of the Surgeon General, Dr. Nadine Burke Harris, a pediatrician, and a trail blazer of our time. We now have the knowledge, resources, and tools to reverse the damage of ACEs.

We are in a perfect storm. In the midst of escalating racial tension, the swell of the Black Lives Matter movement with escalating AAPI Hate, the healing of the societal pain must include the white bodies along with the individuals with black, brown, or rainbow bodies. If you re-call in history, US was once referred as the Paper Tiger.

The Paper Tiger's Daughters is an allegory of AAPI women's plight of America today. I strongly believe that this is a time of awakening to heal as humankind. Starting with the self, follow by family, community, society, country, and the earth. Together we can restore this land, the beautiful country, as the beacon of hope for many generations of immigrants before us. May the spirit of the tiger rise up and carry us collectively to move forth, heal the pain body, dismantle structural racism, and restore human kindness on earth with grace and ease for the greatest good. Namaste.

ABOUT THE AUTHOR

Betsy Chang Ha is a retired nurse and health care executive. She founded CLC Health Collaborative, a mission-focused consulting venture to advance health equity and ameliorate the epigenetic harm of ACEs in partnership with the health and wellness community. The Paper Tiger's Daughters is her first book to tell the AAPI women's story from the intersectionality of cross-generational trauma and multi-ethnic Asian American's immigration experience. The intention of this book is to plant a seed of healing, to help reverse the generational trauma, and to create a kinder world for our future generations. She continues to teach yoga and create art. She lives in Huntington Beach, California with her husband Co.

.

Made in the USA
Middletown, DE
25 July 2022